FOREWORD

"The "DBT Therapy Handbook" is a groundbreaking contribution to the world of mental health. It effortlessly combines theoretical insights with practical applications, creating a comprehensive guide for individuals on their journey towards emotional regulation and mindfulness. This handbook stands as a powerful toolkit to understanding the power of Dialectical Behavior Therapy in transforming lives, making it an indispensable resource for both therapists and individuals committed to their mental well-being." - *Dr. Jessica A. - Clinical Psychologist, USA.*

****

"As a practitioner deeply involved in emotional well-being, I cannot overstate the significance of the "DBT Therapy Handbook." It transcends conventional therapeutic methods, providing a clear and practical understanding of Dialectical Behavior Therapy. The handbook's approach to mindfulness and interpersonal effectiveness is not only informative but genuinely transformative. If you're navigating the intricate rollercoster of emotional troubles, consider this handbook your steadfast companion." - *Therapist Samuel R. - Mindfulness Specialist, UK.*

"Within the vibrant tapestry of mental health literature, the "DBT Therapy Handbook" shines as a beacon of clarity and authenticity. Authored by Dr Anna K.O Jones, this handbook offers more than just knowledge; it extends an invitation to actively engage with the principles of Dialectical Behavior Therapy. Whether you're a professional in the field or an individual seeking personal growth, get ready for a transformative journey guided by the wisdom encapsulated in these pages." - *Dr. Laura M. - Psychotherapist, Canada.*

****

"Hailing from the dynamic mental health landscape in Toronto, Canada, I am honored to endorse the "DBT Therapy Handbook." Driven by a passion for supporting emotional well-being, this handbook is not just a read—it's an immersive experience. With a commitment to authenticity and practicality, it stands as a guide that transcends cultural boundaries, offering invaluable insights into the universality of Dialectical Behavior Therapy." - *Dr. Alex S. - Mental Health Counselor, Canada.*

"Embarking on the journey of emotional well-being requires more than just information; it demands a roadmap crafted with authenticity and expertise. The "DBT Therapy Handbook" delivers on this demand. Authored by Dr Anna K.O Jones who is an expert in the field, this handbook is more than a guide; it's a companion that empowers individuals to master the intricacies of Dialectical Behavior Therapy. Brace yourself for a journey that transcends the pages and becomes a profound exploration of self." - ***Dr. Sofia W. - Psychiatric Nurse Practitioner, Canada.***

COPYRIGHT

© 2024 by Dr Anna K.O Jones

This book is a product of passion, empathy, and countless cups of coffee. Dr Anna K.O Jones invites you to share and savour its pages with an open heart. Feel free to engage in discussions, share insights, and pass the wisdom along – after all, knowledge grows when it's shared.

The author acknowledges the inspiration drawn from the diverse tapestry of human experiences. Every story, every struggle, and every triumph woven into these pages is a celebration of the shared journey we call life.

Cover design by Cliff Global Graphics. The captivating visuals were crafted to mirror the essence of the words within—bold yet gentle, a visual invitation to explore the depths of the human experience.

Published by

Dr. Anna K.O Jones

DISCLAIMER

The insights, guidance, and personal stories shared in this book are offered sincerely to provide support and foster understanding. Dr. Anna K.O Jones, the author, warmly recognises that each reader embarks on a unique journey, and what resonates for one person may not necessarily mirror the experiences of another.

It's important to clarify that this book does not replace professional advice or treatment. While it has been carefully crafted with consideration, readers are strongly encouraged to consult qualified professionals for personalised guidance on their emotional and mental health needs. The publisher invites readers to approach the content of this book with thoughtful contemplation. Any actions taken by readers based on the book's content are the individual's responsibility. The aim is to provide insights that inspire positive reflection, promoting personal autonomy and discernment in applying the information presented.

The perspectives shared within these pages reflect the author's personal experiences and observations. They are not meant to dictate a singular truth but to offer diverse viewpoints, encouraging reflective introspection.

In the spirit of authenticity and acknowledging human imperfection, it's recognised that no book can encompass every nuance of the human experience. Dr Anna K.O Jones hopes this work is a companion on your journey rather than a definitive guide.

Feel free to express your thoughts and experiences inspired by this book. Whether through art, writing, or conversation, your unique expression contributes to the collective tapestry of shared stories.

ABOUT THE AUTHOR

Dr. Anna K.O Jones is multifaceted, seamlessly weaving the roles of a dedicated medical practitioner, a nurturing mother, and a prolific writer. With an unwavering commitment to mental health, she is a beacon of hope and understanding in human emotions and relationships.

As a passionate medical practitioner specialising in mental health, Dr. Jones brings expertise and empathy to her practice. She has over 15 years of experience in helping people cope with various mental health issues, such as anxiety, depression, anger, stress, and self-care. She is also a certified relationship counsellor specialising in communication, conflict resolution, and intimacy. Through years of clinical experience, she has become a trusted guide, helping individuals navigate the complexities of their emotional well-being.

In addition to her clinical pursuits, Dr. Jones is a gifted writer, penning insightful self-help books that resonate with readers worldwide. Her works delve into the depths of the human psyche, offering practical wisdom on managing mental health challenges. Topics range from the intricacies of anxiety and depression to the nuances of anger, stress, and the art of self-care.

Beyond the individual, Dr. Anna K.O Jones is a staunch advocate for healthy relationships. Her literary repertoire extends to interpersonal dynamics, with books exploring communication, conflict resolution, and the delicate balance of intimacy. Through her words, she empowers individuals to forge stronger connections and navigate the intricate dance of human relationships.

Outside the professional sphere, Dr. Jones wears the hat of a loving mother. Her experiences in motherhood add a profound layer to her understanding of the human experience, enriching her personal and professional perspectives. She embodies the delicate art of balancing the demands of a thriving career with the joys and challenges of raising a family.

Dr. Anna K.O Jones's impact extends far beyond the confines of her office and the pages of her books. Her mission is to destigmatise mental health, fostering a world where understanding and compassion prevail. Through her tireless efforts, she continues to touch lives, inspiring individuals to embark on self-discovery and fostering healthier, more fulfilling relationships

TABLE OF CONTENTS

INTRODUCTION

To commence our exploration, we will pose a fundamental question that underpins the entirety of this text: What constitutes dialectical behavior therapy, and what advantages does its application offer? Additionally, we will delve into distinguishing features that set dialectical behavior therapy apart from other widely practiced therapeutic approaches, such as cognitive behavior therapy.

The origins of dialectical behavior therapy can be traced back to the 1980s, anchored in the context of borderline personality disorder. Also known as emotionally unstable personality disorder, the nomenclature itself conveys a significant aspect of the disorder. It manifests as a persistent and deeply ingrained set of characteristics centered around a prevailing sense of emptiness and detachment, coupled with a pervasive fear of abandonment. Individuals grappling with borderline personality disorder often exhibit an unstable self-perception and fluctuating emotions. Concurrently, many individuals with this disorder face additional challenges, including a history of substance abuse, depression, or eating disorders like anorexia or bulimia. Distressingly, those with borderline personality disorder exhibit a heightened vulnerability to suicide, with one in ten individuals succumbing to this tragic fate.

A formidable obstacle in the treatment of individuals with borderline personality disorder stems from the inherent difficulty in medicating personality disorders. Unlike other disorders with identifiable causes, personality disorders lack concrete origins, making it challenging to develop medications targeting a singular root cause. Complicating matters further, borderline personality disorder doesn't exhibit apparent neurological effects that can be easily mitigated by medication. While some evidence suggests its impact on specific brain regions, a definitive method to effectively address the root cause of borderline personality disorder remains elusive. Medication, therefore, can only be prescribed to alleviate peripheral conditions, offering little influence on the core aspects of the disorder.

In response to this challenge, a collaborative effort among medical professionals emerged, focused on developing a treatment method rooted in the existing cognitive behavior therapy framework. This innovative approach would later be coined dialectical behavior therapy, aiming to assimilate established concepts from cognitive behavior therapy while incorporating novel elements derived predominantly from Buddhist practices.

The outcome was the inception of the first psychotherapeutic intervention demonstrated to be generally effective in addressing borderline personality disorder. Significantly, dialectical behavior therapy has also demonstrated utility in assisting individuals facing broader challenges, such as self-harming tendencies or suicidal thoughts.

This specific therapeutic approach distinguishes itself by catering to individuals in a manner unparalleled by most other therapeutic modalities. Its foundation lies in enhancing patients' capacity to regulate their emotions and thoughts by scrutinizing the root causes of their emotional experiences. Dialectical behaviour therapy stands out by systematically evaluating what triggers their emotional responses and empowering them to apply constructive coping mechanisms.

The therapy achieves this by employing various concepts designed to isolate, analyze, and disregard negative thoughts. Dialectical behavior therapy is structured into four discrete modules, executed cyclically to facilitate this process. This structured approach allows for a comprehensive and iterative exploration of the individual's emotional and cognitive landscape, fostering meaningful and sustainable change over time.

The foundation of dialectical behavior therapy rests upon four crucial pillars, each playing a distinct role in fostering emotional well-being and behavioral transformation.

The first cornerstone is mindfulness, arguably the most pivotal element in dialectical behavior therapy, serving as the bedrock that underpins the entire therapeutic process. The cultivation of mindfulness is deemed essential, a topic we will delve into extensively in its dedicated chapter.

Moving on to the second pillar, we encounter distress tolerance. This aspect revolves around an individual's capacity to confront and navigate distressing situations without succumbing to the prevailing trend in mental health treatments that strive to alter such circumstances. Particularly pertinent for those grappling with irrational or self-destructive thought patterns, distress tolerance emphasizes dealing with distressing situations without catalyzing or exacerbating negative behaviors.

The third essential element is emotional regulation, addressing an individual's capability to recognize and manage emotions responsively. It involves developing a heightened sense of detachment and objectivity when dealing with emotional experiences. The chapter dedicated to emotional regulation will comprehensively explore the multifaceted processes involved in building these indispensable skills.

The final pillar is interpersonal effectiveness, focusing on an individual's ability to communicate and interact effectively with others. Often, individuals with borderline personality disorder and related challenges may articulate how situations should be handled but struggle to implement these strategies when actively engaged. Interpersonal effectiveness in dialectical behavior therapy strives to bridge this gap, fostering improved communication and relationship management skills.

These four concepts operate cyclically, each contributing to the holistic benefits of dialectical behavior therapy.

The dynamic interaction between the therapist and the patient lies at the heart of dialectical behavior therapy. This therapeutic model emphasizes a highly supportive role for the therapist, extending accessibility outside formal therapy sessions if required to provide ongoing emotional support.

Furthermore, the patient is encouraged to view the therapist not as an adversary but as a friend. To establish this relationship dynamic, therapists aim to validate the patient's feelings while constructively addressing negative behaviors. The intent is to guide the patient towards more effective coping strategies, fostering an environment of acceptance, support, and mutual collaboration in pursuing positive change.

The ultimate objective of dialectical behavior therapy sessions is for the patient to attain what they define as a "life worth living." This encompasses not only the transformation of existing behaviors but also the cultivation of new, positive behaviors.

Given the pronounced emphasis on establishing a therapeutic relationship between an individual and a therapist in dialectical behavior therapy, a pertinent question arises: Is it a realistic approach to attempt this therapy independently? The unequivocal answer is yes, it is indeed realistic. However, the caveat is that it necessitates substantial effort on the individual's part. By the conclusion of this journey, individuals should ideally harness the principles of dialectical behavior therapy to effectively manage relationships, address disorders, and alleviate general malaise.

This book provides the requisite structure to engage in dialectical behavior therapy autonomously. It acknowledges the considerable effort required while assuring that, through commitment, you can utilize dialectical behavior therapy as a valuable tool in your personal development.

While the primary focus is on self-application, a dedicated chapter offers guidance for helping others using the methods outlined in this book. If you choose to act as a "therapist" for someone else, it is imperative to be mentally prepared for the challenges they may present. Genuine acceptance is crucial for them to feel a sense of camaraderie in the process. The worst-case scenario inadvertently impeded their progress, highlighting the importance of approaching this role with the necessary understanding and empathy.

Now that you've grasped the essence of dialectical behavior therapy and determined it as your preferred approach, the question arises: How can you maximize the benefits of this system? How can you integrate dialectical behavior therapy into your daily life?

First and foremost, it's crucial to recognize that dialectical behavior therapy doesn't overwhelm you with all its components simultaneously. Instead, the method follows a structured approach, emphasizing one of the four methodologies behind dialectical behavior therapy during specific periods.

SECTION ONE: UNDERSTANDING THE CONCEPTS OF DIALECTICAL BEHAVIOR THERAPY

Dialectical behavior therapy (DBT) represents a distinctive pattern of psychotherapy characterized by a cognitive-behavioral approach, with a pronounced focus on psychosocial treatments. Unlike other therapeutic modalities, DBT emphasizes understanding and addressing the variations in individuals' reactions to emotional situations.

At its core, DBT operates on the fundamental premise that people's responses to emotional stimuli are not universally uniform; instead, they exhibit significant variations. In the context of romantic and interpersonal relationships, some individuals respond intensely to emotional situations, while others do not manifest the same level of intensity. The theoretical underpinning of DBT suggests that specific individuals experience rapid arousal, reaching higher levels of emotional stimulation more quickly than their counterparts. Simultaneously, these individuals take comparatively more time than average to return to baseline or standard arousal levels.

Individuals exhibiting these tendencies are often diagnosed with borderline personality disorder, a condition marked by extreme and abrupt fluctuations in emotion. Understandably, these individuals face challenges in conveying their emotional experiences to those around them, leading to crises within familial and childhood environments. DBT emerges as a therapeutic method specifically designed to impart skills essential for coping with sudden and intense emotional surges.

While DBT falls under the broader category of cognitive-behavioral approaches, it possesses critical and distinctive elements that set it apart from other variants within this therapeutic paradigm. Recognizing these unique components is imperative for a treatment to be classified as or incorporate DBT effectively. The method's holistic approach addresses the symptoms and underlying causes, offering individuals a comprehensive strategy for managing their emotional experiences and promoting lasting positive change.

The Components And Characteristics Of Dialectical Behavior Therapy Treatments

Dialectical behavioral treatment (DBT), distinct from other therapeutic approaches, is characterized by five essential functions: individual therapy, group therapy, and a therapist consultation team. This multi-faceted structure distinguishes DBT as a comprehensive treatment program rather than a singular intervention conducted by any practitioner. The nuanced and intricate nature of DBT sets it apart, involving various processes in its application, making it a challenging yet highly effective therapeutic model. This comprehensive approach may pose difficulties for some clinicians interested in implementing DBT.

To successfully implement DBT, it is crucial to understand and meticulously address the five key treatment functions, as they constitute the cornerstone of any DBT program.

Despite the substantial empirical support for DBT, its application and implementation can vary based on different settings and circumstances that may arise in the process.

Consequently, the flexibility of DBT allows for innovative and creative applications in response to diverse situations.

<u>*The five critical functions of treatment in DBT encompass:*</u>

Enhancing Motivation and Mitigating Dysfunctional Behavior: Individuals grappling with borderline personality disorder often face challenges in mustering the motivation to undergo transformative changes and relinquish life-threatening patterns and habits. Consequently, a pivotal role of Dialectical Behavior Therapy (DBT) is to elevate motivation and propel patients toward shedding unhealthy and perilous behaviors. This crucial facet of DBT is primarily addressed within the context of individual therapy, employing a meticulous monitoring approach.

In individual therapy sessions, therapists guide patients to document various treatment targets using a diary card, a self-monitoring tool. The spectrum of treatment targets varies across individuals and may encompass self-harm, suicidal tendencies, emotional complexities, and more. The diary card serves a dual purpose, aiding therapists in prioritizing and scheduling therapy sessions.

Prioritization of sessions is structured based on the severity of threats, with immediate life-threatening behaviors such as suicidal attempts taking precedence over behaviors that, while not immediately life-threatening, may impede therapeutic progress. Such hindering behaviors include delinquency, unemployment, and disorders obstructing the patient's well-being.

Once prioritization is complete, therapy sessions commence with the therapist assisting patients in dissecting the identified behaviors' reasons, effects, and consequences.
Furthermore, the therapist collaborates with the patient to apply skillful and practical strategies to address life challenges and navigate emotional regulation. Incorporating commitment strategies, the therapist instills encouragement and motivation within the patient, fostering a positive trajectory toward meaningful change. This comprehensive and tailored approach within DBT strives not only to rectify behaviors but also to nurture intrinsic motivation for sustained and constructive transformation.

Enhancing Your Capacities: There is a prevalent assumption that individuals grappling with borderline personality disorder must enhance essential skills vital for their everyday lives and interpersonal relationships. These pivotal skills include regulating emotions effectively, maintaining balance, cultivating mindfulness to engage with present experiences attentively, and fostering proficient interpersonal skills to navigate relationships adeptly.

Developing adequate distress tolerance skills is also imperative for navigating stress and pressure without exacerbating situations.

Consequently, a pivotal function of Dialectical Behavior Therapy (DBT) is enhancing and equipping patients with these indispensable skills.

This vital function within DBT primarily unfolds through group therapy sessions, serving as the mechanism to impart, practice, and reinforce these crucial skills. In these group sessions, patients are not only taught the necessary skills but are also provided with opportunities to practice them. To reinforce the integration of these skills into daily life, clients are assigned homework assignments, promoting the practical application and mastery of the acquired skills beyond the confines of the therapy setting. This comprehensive approach within DBT strives to empower individuals with the practical tools necessary for improved emotional regulation, interpersonal effectiveness, and adept navigation of life's challenges.

Dialectical Behavior Therapy (DBT) encompasses four foundational skill training components systematically imparted to clients during therapy sessions. These units, modules, or training components play a pivotal role in equipping individuals with practical tools for improved well-being:

Mindfulness: The skills under the mindfulness unit focus on enhancing clients' ability to pay non-judgmental attention to present situations. By cultivating mindfulness, clients develop a heightened awareness of the current moment, fostering a more transparent and objective understanding of their experiences.

Interpersonal Effectiveness: This unit concentrates on developing and refining clients' problem-solving abilities and interpersonal skills. By honing these competencies, clients acquire the tools to navigate and enhance their interactions with others, fostering more effective and constructive relationships.

Emotional Regulation: Aimed at addressing the heightened emotional states commonly experienced by individuals with borderline personality traits, this unit equips clients with essential emotional regulation skills. These skills include recognizing and labelling emotions identifying obstacles to changing emotional states, reducing vulnerability to emotional fluctuations, deliberately engaging in positive activities, increasing mindfulness and rationality in the present moment, taking proactive measures against negative emotions, and applying distress tolerance techniques to handle pressure and challenging situations effectively.

Distress Tolerance: Distress tolerance skills empower clients to make informed and wise decisions when faced with pressure and distressing situations. Rather than succumbing to overwhelming emotions, these skills enable individuals to confront challenges directly, preventing the burying of problems within themselves and fostering resilience in the face of adversity.

These four core skill training components collectively form the backbone of DBT, providing clients with a comprehensive toolkit to navigate the complexities of their emotions, relationships, and daily life challenges.

Ensuring Applicability in Everyday Life: The efficacy of therapy is contingent upon the practical integration of acquired skills into patients' daily lives. If this integration is lacking, the therapy may be deemed unsuccessful. A pivotal and critical role of Dialectical Behavior Therapy (DBT) lies in generalizing treatment results and gains. This crucial function is achieved during skill training by actively involving patients in homework assignments and providing a real-world platform to test and apply their newly acquired or enhanced skills.

This process systematically addresses identified problems and defects, offering tailored solutions to augment the patients' skill set. Beyond structured skill training, individual therapy sessions play a vital role in monitoring and facilitating the application of acquired skills and other benefits from therapy in patients' everyday lives. Within these sessions, therapists actively assist patients in applying the newly developed or improved skills to navigate real-life situations. Patients are encouraged to practice these skills and behaviors, promoting the practical assimilation of therapeutic benefits.

Moreover, therapists aim to maintain continuous availability, ensuring a support system for patients in crises. Whether through phone consultations or other efficient means, therapists remain accessible to provide urgent assistance, reinforcing the ongoing integration of learned skills beyond the confines of therapy sessions. This comprehensive approach within DBT prioritizes the practical applicability of skills, ultimately contributing to meaningful improvements in patients' daily lives.

SECTION TWO: THE APPLICATIONS OF DIALECTICAL BEHAVIOR THERAPY

DBT proves most beneficial for individuals navigating intense emotional experiences, often finding themselves quickly overwhelmed by life's challenges and relational stressors. The point of distress reaches such an extent that they perceive their emotional responses as unmanageable.

Consequently, they resort to impulsive actions to momentarily alleviate their distress, unaware that these reactions exacerbate their long-term problems.

Originally designed to assist those diagnosed with Borderline Personality Disorder (BPD), DBT has proven highly effective in treating individuals facing severe mood swings and struggling to employ coping strategies against intense and sudden emotional urges. Beyond BPD, DBT has successfully aided individuals dealing with severe depression, PTSD, eating disorders, compulsive disorders, Bipolar Disorder, ADHD, anger management issues, and substance abuse. Notably, DBT has demonstrated effectiveness in helping those engaged in self-harm as a coping mechanism for intense emotional troubles.

To gain insights into the profile of individuals who thrive in DBT, it is essential to explore common characteristics shared by this group. Successful DBT participants typically exhibit a high level of emotional vulnerability, manifesting as a predisposition to experience emotions reactively and intensely. This heightened emotional reactivity might be inherent, with some individuals being naturally wired to feel emotions more intensely than the average person. DBT theory proposes that the automatic nervous system of emotionally vulnerable individuals is prone to heightened reactivity even to low-stress levels, and their nervous system takes longer to return to baseline after stress removal.

Moreover, some individuals within this category may grapple with mood disorders like major depression or generalized anxiety, impacting how intensely they experience emotions. Consequently, emotionally vulnerable individuals often find themselves caught in a perpetual roller coaster of quick, intense emotional reactions that prove challenging to control throughout their lives.

Clinicians have observed that individuals seeking DBT treatment for heightened emotional vulnerability are not solely predisposed to intense emotions or mood disorders. Typically, these individuals have also endured prolonged exposure to invalidating environments, often originating in early childhood but potentially occurring at any stage of life. These environments failed to offer the necessary support, attention, respect, or understanding for individuals to effectively navigate their emotions. Invalidating environments encompass a broad spectrum, ranging from situations involving severe emotional or physical abuse to mismatches in parent-child personalities.

Consider the scenario of a reserved child born or adopted into a family dominated by extroverted individuals, subjecting them to constant teasing about their introverted nature. Alternatively, envision a child with ADIID facing inflexible parents prone to frequent yelling. Both examples illustrate invalidating environments where the individual, already predisposed to heightened emotional experiences, lacks the support and validation needed. Consequently, being placed in such environments makes them even more emotionally vulnerable.

In these circumstances, individuals may exhibit increased emotional reactivity as they inadvertently learn that their feelings are only taken seriously when expressed in an extremely emotional manner. The lack of support or validation in invalidating environments exacerbates their emotional vulnerability, fostering a pattern of heightened emotional responsiveness to navigate an environment that fails to acknowledge their emotional needs.

Let's illustrate the impact of an invalidating environment using the example of an introverted boy, constantly told by his father to "man up" and adopt a more aggressive approach to life. Feeling ridiculed, the boy began to question himself and on one occasion, when his father addressed him, he uncontrollably burst into tears. Surprisingly, his father's demeanor immediately shifted, and his mother rushed to give him abundant attention. This pattern repeated itself, creating an interesting dynamic. The boy's unconscious mind started to recognize a sequence: 'My dad harasses me, I cry uncontrollably, the harassment stops, and I receive lots of attention.' As the boy noticed the effectiveness of this pattern, he began to employ it more frequently, with each successful demonstration inadvertently reinforcing the behavior. Gradually, his emotional outbursts became validated, evolving into an ingrained coping skill.

Unbeknownst to the boy, this process unconsciously reinforced his emotional vulnerability, exacerbating it over time. This pattern is commonly observed in individuals with conditions like Borderline Personality Disorder, Bipolar Disorder, eating disorders, and other disorders effectively treated with DBT. The subsequent section will provide an overview of several disorders successfully addressed through DBT.

Borderline Personality Disorder And Its Difficult Characteristics

People diagnosed with Borderline Personality Disorder (BPD) undergo heightened and prolonged emotional experiences compared to the general population. They frequently engage in persistent and chronic emotional outbursts, leading mental health professionals to characterize this group as consistently navigating a state of crisis. Their default mode tends to be crisis-oriented due to a lack of acquired coping mechanisms necessary to manage their intense emotions effectively.

Emotionally, individuals with BPD are more susceptible, requiring an extended duration to return to a baseline state following emotional events.

Therapists have identified a typical pattern among individuals with BPD: adopting the belief system of the invalidating environment they are exposed. This inclination leads to "self-invalidation," wherein they dismiss their emotions and problem-solving abilities.

Additionally, they often form unrealistic expectations, feeling shame and anger when unable to meet personal goals or when confronted with challenges.

Another characteristic of those with BPD is their inclination to impose inflexible and impractical demands on themselves and others. When faced with deviations from their plans or desires, they frequently resort to "blaming." This cognitive error involves attributing responsibility for their problems to external factors, making it challenging for them to acknowledge the need for personal behavioral changes to achieve different outcomes in their lives.

Individuals with Borderline Personality Disorder (BPD) may resort to self-harm, such as cutting, or exhibit suicidal tendencies as coping mechanisms for their intense emotional distress. Suicidal tendencies often manifest in emotionally vulnerable individuals who react strongly to severe trauma, whether it be physical or emotional abuse, prompting contemplation of suicide as a way to escape ongoing pain. Seeking relief, they may attempt suicide and, upon hospitalization, receive significant attention, leading to a newfound sense of validation and acknowledgment.

Individuals with BPD commonly struggle with a poor sense of self and face challenges in forming and maintaining interpersonal relationships. They often seek out individuals willing to take charge and solve their problems, allowing them to avoid taking responsibility. Despite projecting an image of competence, they wear a mask to appear capable of handling their problems and emotions independently. While they may excel in certain aspects of life, they struggle to generalize this competence to other areas.

The lifestyle created by most individuals with BPD, coupled with their difficulty in returning to baseline emotions after an event, exposes them to ongoing traumatic experiences. Moreover, their avoidance of negative emotions, even healthy ones, stems from a lack of regulation skills. Consequently, they find themselves overwhelmed and unprepared when faced with emotionally challenging situations, leading to prolonged and intense emotional states.

Take, for instance, the young individual who resorts to self-harm, like cutting or burning, as a means of finding momentary relief. When others discover these actions, there's a sudden shift in how they perceive and respond to him. Much like the scenario described earlier, he starts to experience a sense of validation.

Now, what unfolds in these situations? In both cases, these individuals persist in such behaviors over time. Why? Because it's during these moments that they feel acknowledged and supported, turning these actions into ingrained coping mechanisms.

Bipolar Disorder: Symptoms And Types

This condition is often colloquially referred to as Manic Depressive Disorder due to the individual's tendency to oscillate between manic episodes and more depressive states. It is characterized by significant and unusual fluctuations in activity levels, energy, mood, and daily task performance. These symptoms, unlike typical mood changes, are severe and extreme, impacting relationships, work or school performance, and even leading to suicidal contemplation.

As is typical with psychological disorders, there is typically no singular cause for Bipolar Disorder. Instead, it often arises from a combination of biological and environmental factors, acting together to either trigger or elevate the risk of the disorder.

Genetics plays a role, with research identifying specific genes that may influence its development. Familial patterns also indicate a higher likelihood of the disorder in children from certain families or those with a sibling already affected.

However, environmental factors also contribute significantly. Studies involving identical twins, who share identical genetic makeup, reveal that if one twin develops the disorder, the other does not always, suggesting the influence of non-genetic triggers.

Individuals with Bipolar Disorder undergo intense emotional states known as "mood episodes," each lasting for varying durations. Manic episodes are characterized by heightened activity and extreme joy, while depressive episodes involve feelings of sadness, dysphoria, hopelessness, and sometimes irritability. A "mixed state" occurs when characteristics of both manic and depressive episodes coexist simultaneously.

Here are symptoms commonly associated with Bipolar Disorder:

Manic Episode:

- Prolonged periods of feeling "high" or pleased
- Rapid speech and jumping between ideas, indicative of racing thoughts
- Easy distractibility
- Increased activity levels and initiation of numerous new projects
- Restlessness
- Limited need for sleep
- Unrealistic beliefs about one's capabilities
- Impulsiveness and fixation on pleasurable and risky activities

Depressive Episode:

- Extended periods of extreme irritability
- Prolonged feelings of sadness or hopelessness
- Loss of interest in once-enjoyed activities
- Fatigue and a sense of sluggishness
- Challenges in memory, concentration, and decision-making
- Alterations in eating, sleeping, and other habitual patterns

- Presence of suicidal thoughts, gestures, and/or attempts may also occur

Bipolar Disorder. Without proper treatment, hypomania might progress to full mania or other symptoms of Bipolar Disorder.

As previously mentioned, Bipolar Disorder can also present in a mixed state, where an individual experiences both depression and mania simultaneously. In this state, one may feel disturbed, have disrupted sleep, lose appetite, and even contemplate suicide, all while experiencing a sense of hopelessness or sadness along with heightened energy.

During severe episodes of depression or mania, individuals may encounter psychotic symptoms like delusions or hallucinations, which intensify their extreme mood swings. For instance, in a manic episode, someone might believe they possess presidential authority, immense wealth, or special powers. In depressive episodes, individuals may harbor delusions of homelessness, ruin, poverty, or criminality. Unfortunately, misdiagnoses with schizophrenia or other reality testing disorders can occur due to mood-induced hallucinations.

Individuals with Bipolar Disorder frequently contend with co-occurring conditions like polysubstance abuse or dependence, anxiety disorders (e.g., PTSD and phobias), and occasionally, Attention Deficit Hyperactivity Disorder (ADHD). Additionally, they face a higher likelihood of physical ailments such as diabetes, headaches, thyroid disease, heart disease, migraines, obesity, and other health issues.

Typically emerging in late teenage years or early adulthood, Bipolar Disorder may show initial symptoms in childhood or develop later in life. A significant portion of cases begins before the age of 25.

There are several types of Bipolar Disorder, each with its distinct characteristics:

Bipolar I Disorder: Involves at least one manic episode, which may be preceded or followed by hypomanic or major depressive episodes.
The manic episodes are severe and can significantly impact daily functioning.

Bipolar II Disorder: Characterized by recurring episodes of major depression and hypomania.

Unlike Bipolar I, individuals with Bipolar II never experience full-blown manic episodes.

Bipolar Disorder Not Otherwise Specified (BP-NOS): This category is used when symptoms don't precisely fit the criteria for Bipolar I or II but still involve significant mood swings.

Cyclothymic Disorder or Cyclothymia: A chronic condition involving numerous periods of hypomanic symptoms and depressive symptoms.

However, the symptoms are less severe and don't meet the criteria for major depressive or hypomanic episodes. These classifications help in understanding and diagnosing the varying presentations of Bipolar Disorder based on the nature and intensity of mood episodes.

Without proper diagnosis and treatment, Bipolar Disorder can worsen over time. The condition tends to become more severe as episodes increase in frequency. This escalation can lead to behaviors that profoundly affect various aspects of life, including relationships, personal goals, finances, housing, work, and school.

Dialectical Behavioral Therapy (DBT) has proven to be effective in assisting individuals with Bipolar Disorder to lead healthier and more productive lives. DBT interventions have often contributed to reducing the severity and frequency of bipolar episodes. This therapeutic approach helps individuals develop coping skills, regulate emotions, and manage the challenges associated with Bipolar Disorder, fostering improved overall well-being.

Post-Traumatic Stress Disorder

The human body is equipped with an inherent mechanism designed to respond to danger, known as the fight-or-flight response. When the brain signals imminent danger, the body automatically enters a response mode, inducing fear and preparing for either fleeing to safety or fighting for self-preservation. This natural biological process is crucial for protecting individuals from harm. However, in some cases, repeated exposure to trauma or a single intense traumatic experience can disrupt this normal response, leading to an abnormal state known as Post-Traumatic Stress Disorder (PTSD).

PTSD typically arises after an individual has undergone a terrifying or life-threatening ordeal, often involving actual physical harm or the threat of harm. The traumatic event might have affected the person directly, or a loved one, or could have been witnessed by the individual. Instances that can trigger PTSD include:

- ☐ Rape or sexual abuse
- ☐ Terrorism
- ☐ Robbery
- ☐ Train wrecks
- ☐ Car accidents
- ☐ Plane crashes
- ☐ Natural disasters like floods, earthquakes, and tornadoes
- ☐ Childhood physical abuse
- ☐ Domestic violence
- ☐ Hostage situations
- ☐ War
- ☐ Torture
- ☐ Bombings
- ☐ Any other highly traumatic events

PTSD arises from a combination of genetic and environmental factors. The individual's biological predisposition to handling fear sensations and memories significantly contributes to the development of PTSD. Those whose brain chemistry makes them more emotionally vulnerable to fear are at a higher risk of developing PTSD.

Environmental influences play a crucial role in PTSD onset. Traumatic experiences in childhood, head injuries, or a personal history of mental illness can elevate the likelihood of developing the disorder. Personality and cognitive factors, encompassing thinking errors, distress tolerance, pessimism, and other cognitive aspects, also contribute to increased risk. Additionally, social factors, such as the presence of a support system, aid in coping with trauma and may serve as a protective factor against the development of PTSD.

The Undiscussed Symptoms Of PTSD You Must Know

Symptoms of PTSD fall into three distinct categories:

The Hyperarousal Symptoms: Individuals recovering from PTSD often exhibit hyperarousal symptoms, characterized by increased sensitivity and tension compared to their pre-traumatic state. Their heightened autonomic nervous system activity results in difficulties sleeping and managing anger, leading to frequent angry outbursts. It's crucial to note that hyperarousal symptoms persist consistently and may manifest without a specific trigger.

It is natural for individuals to experience one or several of these symptoms following a traumatic event. However, it's important to recognize that children and teenagers may display different reactions to PTSD. In younger children, observable signs may include reverting to bedwetting after being potty trained, not speaking despite reaching verbal developmental milestones, or reenacting the traumatic event during play.

Symptoms may align more closely with those observed in adults for older children and adolescents. Additionally, there might be an increase in disrespectful and explosive behavior, alongside a preoccupation with seeking revenge or feelings of guilt for not preventing the traumatic event or associated injuries.

PTSD can occur at any age, with females having a higher risk, and a significant genetic link is observed. Not everyone who undergoes a risky event develops PTSD. Various factors determine the likelihood of an individual developing PTSD, with those increasing the risk termed as risk factors and those lowering the chances as resilience factors. Some of these factors are present before the trauma, while others emerge during or after a traumatic event.

The Re-experiencing symptoms:

- Flashbacks, vividly reliving the traumatic event.
- Nightmares related to the distressing experience.
- Intrusive and persistent frightening thoughts that emerge unexpectedly, proving challenging to dismiss.

These re-experiencing symptoms can significantly disrupt daily functioning, posing challenges in routine activities and interpersonal relationships.

The Avoidance Symptoms: Individuals with PTSD may exhibit avoidance symptoms as a coping mechanism to shield themselves from the emotional impact of a traumatic incident. This avoidance extends to anything that serves as a reminder of the traumatic event, as approaching such stimuli triggers an overwhelming emotional response.

Emotional numbness is another manifestation of avoidance symptoms. Rather than risk experiencing intense negative emotions, individuals may choose emotional numbness, avoiding any emotional engagement to evade negative feelings altogether. Strong feelings of worry, depression, or guilt without clear reasons are also indicative of avoidant symptoms. Instead of addressing the incident directly, individuals with PTSD may experience generalized negative emotions.

A notable avoidant symptom is a loss of interest in previously enjoyable activities. People with PTSD tend to avoid engaging in any pleasurable activities. Difficulties in recalling the traumatic incident are common, as some individuals find it easier to suppress the entire experience into their subconscious, representing a form of avoidance.

Changes in routine also reflect avoidant tendencies. In some cases, individuals deliberately alter their routines to avoid potential triggers. For example, a person might refrain from driving a car after a life-threatening accident or avoid air travel following a traumatic event, as witnessed after the terrorist attacks.

Protective Factors For PTSD

- Availability of a sufficient support network post-trauma.
- Possession of effective coping mechanisms.
- Maintaining a positive self-perception during challenging times.
- Engagement in therapy or counseling focusing on post-traumatic adjustment.

Risk Factors for PTSD:

- Exposure to a traumatic event.
- Previous history of mental health issues.
- Physical injuries sustained.
- Witnessing harm or death to others.

- Insufficient or absence of social support following an incident.
- Experiencing a loss of home, employment, or a loved one.

Eating Disorders

Certainly, here is a paraphrased version:

An eating disorder is a medical condition characterized by irregular eating habits. However, it transcends a mere disruption in food intake, as individuals grappling with an eating disorder often experience profound distress regarding their body weight and/or shape. To regulate their appearance and enhance their self-perception, those with eating disorders may adopt significantly reduced eating patterns and develop an obsession with exercise. This disturbance in emotions and behavior is not limited to a specific gender and can profoundly impact the individual's physical and emotional well-being.

While eating disorders can manifest at any stage of development, they typically arise during adolescence or early adulthood, frequently coexisting with other psychological and behavioral conditions such as substance abuse, mood disorders, and anxiety disorders.

The subsequent section delves into the three most prevalent types of eating disorders.

Anorexia Nervosa: Individuals grappling with anorexia nervosa often harbor a profound preoccupation with their weight. Fueled by distorted and unrealistic perceptions of their body image, they harbor a deep-seated fear of weight gain and frequently resist maintaining a healthy body weight. Many individuals afflicted by this disorder severely restrict their food intake, reaching a point where their caloric consumption cannot sustain their overall well-being. Despite becoming visibly underweight and raising concerns among observers, they persist in perceiving themselves as overweight. Anorexia can give rise to severe health complications, including infertility, heart issues, organ failure, brain damage, and bone loss, posing a significant risk of mortality for those affected.

Binge Eating Disorder: Individuals grappling with binge eating often experience a loss of control over their eating habits but do not engage in purging behaviors as seen in bulimia. Consequently, many individuals dealing with binge eating may also contend with obesity, leading to increased health-related issues, including heart disease. Similar to those with other eating disorders, individuals facing this disorder often battle intense feelings of shame, guilt, embarrassment, and a sense of loss of control.

The development of eating disorders is believed to be multifaceted, involving complex factors. Contributing elements include biological, psychological, and environmental factors such as irregular hormone functions and genetic predisposition, nutritional deficiencies, negative body image, poor self-esteem, dysfunctional family dynamics, professions, and careers that promote excessive thinness (e.g., modeling), sports that emphasize thinness for performance (e.g., gymnastics, wrestling, long-distance running), childhood sexual abuse, societal pressure to be thin from family, peers, and media, as well as transitions and life changes.

Bulimia Nervosa: Individuals contending with bulimia nervosa commonly grapple with a fear of being overweight and a pervasive dissatisfaction with their body's appearance. This disorder is characterized by a recurring cycle of binge eating followed by compensatory actions to counteract the binge. For instance, an individual may consume excessive amounts of food in a single sitting and subsequently engage in forced vomiting, intense exercise, or the excessive use of laxatives and diuretics, or a combination of these compensatory behaviors. This cycle is typically concealed due to feelings of shame, guilt, and a perceived lack of self-control. Bulimia can result in various health issues, including gastrointestinal problems, dehydration, and heart complications arising from electrolyte imbalances caused by the recurring eating-purging cycle.

Signs and indications of an individual grappling with an eating disorder encompass:

1. Persistent and excessive dieting, even when the person is already underweight.
2. Preoccupation with tracking caloric intake and the fat content of foods.
3. Adoption of ritualistic eating patterns, which might involve solitary eating, breaking food into small pieces, or concealing food for future consumption.
4. Fixation on food, where individuals may intricately prepare elaborate meals for others but abstain from consuming the food themselves.
5. Possible coexisting symptoms of depression or lethargy.

While Dialectical Behavior Therapy (DBT) has demonstrated considerable effectiveness in treating

eating disorders, individuals may require supplementary support in the initial stages of therapy. This support may involve medical monitoring by a physician to address emerging health issues and collaboration with a nutritionist until weight stabilization is achieved. The nutritionist may devise a personalized meal plan to facilitate a return to a healthy weight.

Obsessive-Compulsive Disorder (OCD)

This psychological disorder, if left untreated, can significantly impede individuals, subjecting them to an incessant loop of repetitive behaviors and thoughts. They find themselves overwhelmed by uncontrollable thoughts, fears, and images, leading to continuous obsession. The resulting anxiety compels these individuals to urgently perform specific rituals, routines, or safety-seeking actions as a means to alleviate the distress associated with obsessive thoughts.

While these compulsive behaviors may provide temporary relief, they evolve into chronic issues as individuals must repeatedly engage in the rituals when obsessive thoughts resurface. This ongoing cycle of Obsessive-Compulsive Disorder (OCD) profoundly affects personal relationships and overall well-being. Individuals with OCD often dedicate substantial amounts of time, which would otherwise be spent on regular activities, to fulfill these ritualistic tasks. Despite being aware of the unrealistic and problematic nature of their rituals, individuals with OCD find themselves unable to break free from these patterns.

Frequent obsessions encompass

- Fear of dirt
- Fear of causing harm to others
- Fear of making a mistake
- Fear of being embarrassed
- Fear of behaving in a socially unacceptable manner
- Fear of thinking thoughts that are sinful or evil
- Excessive doubt and the need for constant reassurance

Common compulsions involve

- Repeating specific prayers, phrases, or words
- Washing hands, showering, or bathing repeatedly
- Eating in a certain order
- Having to do errands a specific number of times
- Avoiding touching doorknobs or shaking hands

Major or clinical depression is diagnosed in almost twice as many women as men, leading to a higher likelihood of women undergoing treatment. Biologically vulnerable women face an increased risk due to hormonal changes, pregnancy, miscarriage, menopause, and environmental stressors such as work or home-related pressures, managing family life alongside a career, and caring for aging parents. Single parenthood has also been associated with an elevated risk of depression.

The underreporting of major depression in men is a significant factor contributing to the higher diagnosis rate in women. Men are less likely to report symptoms, and clinical depression in men is unfortunately often overlooked or not disclosed. This reluctance to seek help or discuss their experiences further exacerbates the underrepresentation of depression in men.

Those grappling with the disorders outlined in this section encounter considerable challenges in regulating their emotions, often compounded by social factors contributing to the disorder's manifestation. Dialectical Behavior Therapy (DBT) incorporates psychosocial components, a consideration present in traditional Cognitive Behavioral Therapies (CBT). The primary aim of DBT is to assist individuals in acquiring skills to manage their overwhelming emotions and behaviors effectively. Subsequent chapters will illustrate two DBT models focusing on acceptance and two emphasizing change, fostering a sense of validation and motivation for necessary behavioral adjustments.

SECTION THREE: THE FUNDAMENTAL DIALECTICAL BEHAVIOR THERAPY SKILLS

DBT Distress Tolerance Skills

The Distress Tolerance Skills segment within Dialectical Behavior Therapy (DBT) recognizes the predisposition of certain individuals towards manifesting negative behaviors. It acknowledges that, for such individuals, these behaviors may prove overpowering, necessitating immediate attention. Individuals with this inclination often find themselves overwhelmed even in the face of minimal stress, leading to negative behavioral patterns. While many conventional treatment approaches emphasize evading distressing situations for such individuals, the distress intolerance module adopts a different strategy.

In contrast to the conventional approach of steering clear of painful circumstances, the distress intolerance module encourages clients to acknowledge the inevitability of experiencing pain. The focal point of this approach lies in accepting situations as they are and cultivating the ability to endure the associated discomfort. At the core of the distress tolerance module is the concept of radical acceptance – surrendering to the reality of a stressful moment and recognizing the inability to alter it. Through the practice of radical acceptance, devoid of resistance or judgment towards reality, clients fortify themselves against the development of prolonged and intensely negative emotions.

Fundamentally, the distress tolerance module in DBT encompasses four distinct skills. These skills are designed to equip individuals with the tools to navigate challenging situations, allowing them to endure distress without exacerbating its impact.

This skill comprises of the following:

Self-soothing: The Self-Soothing module within Dialectical Behavior Therapy (DBT) is dedicated to instilling a sense of self-respect and kindness. Its primary objective is to guide individuals in nurturing a positive self-image by engaging their five senses. This involves various activities aimed at fostering self-soothing, each corresponding to a specific sense. Examples include appreciating a scenic view from the window (vision), relishing the sounds of nature, such as birds chirping (hearing), igniting a scented candle (smell), savoring a delightful meal (taste), and experiencing tactile comfort through petting an animal (touch).

The distraction skill: The essence of this skill lies in employing self-directed tools to alleviate irritability and stress in clients. Mastery of self-soothing is a significant achievement within the broader distress tolerance module of DBT. Through self-soothing, individuals extend care, kindness, and compassion to themselves. This not only aids in the immediate calming of distress but also contributes to the development of resilience, facilitating a smoother rebound from challenging situations.

The Distracting module within Dialectical Behavior Therapy (DBT) is a valuable tool for clients to redirect their attention away from distressing emotions and thoughts, engaging in neutral or more enjoyable activities. This approach involves immersing oneself in various endeavors to create a mental and emotional shift, such as pursuing a hobby, taking a brief stroll in the garden, assisting others, or indulging in a movie. These activities aim to foster a sense of detachment from the immediate distress or a troubled state of mind.

To guide individuals in practicing the skill of distraction, the acronym "ACCEPTS" is employed, delineating different facets of this technique:

Activities – Involves the use of positive activities to navigate through a distressing situation.

Contribute – Encourages individuals to assist others in their surroundings or community.

Comparisons – Suggests comparing oneself to individuals facing more challenging circumstances or reflecting on one's past difficulties.

Emotions – Focuses on inducing a shift in emotional states by engaging in activities that evoke happiness or humor.

Push away – Involves temporarily setting aside the distressing situation, mentally pushing it to the background, and substituting it with less stressful thoughts or activities.

Thoughts – Prompts individuals to divert their minds from distressing thoughts by consciously shifting focus to other subjects.

Sensations – Advocates engaging in intense activities to elicit different feelings from the current distress, such as consuming a spicy meal or taking a cold shower.

By employing distraction techniques, individuals can effectively distance themselves from overwhelming emotions, contributing to a sense of relief and allowing for a temporary respite from the distressing situation or mental state

Concentrating on the merit and demerits: The skill centered on Focusing on Pros and Cons involves the creation of a comprehensive list delineating the advantages of enduring a stressful event compared to the drawbacks associated with not tolerating it, potentially resorting to self-destructive behaviors as a coping mechanism. The core purpose is to prompt individuals to recall instances where avoiding confrontation in challenging situations led to adverse consequences. By juxtaposing the positive outcomes of tolerating present stressors against the negative repercussions of succumbing to self-destructive behaviors, this exercise aims to cultivate an awareness of the potential impact on well-being.

This reflective process facilitates a realization of the adverse effects that avoiding confrontation may have had in the past. It is a powerful tool to underscore the importance of developing the capacity to endure current stress without resorting to negative behaviors. Patients can gain insight into the long-term benefits of embracing distress tolerance by highlighting the contrast between constructive coping strategies and impulsive reactions. Ultimately, the objective is to empower individuals to make informed and rational decisions when faced with stress, mitigating the tendency towards impulsive and harmful responses.

The Improving the Moment skill is designed to harness positive mental forces to enhance self-perception. This technique, encapsulated by the acronym IMPROVE, offers a structured approach to cultivating a more positive and resilient mindset:

Imagery – Involves the visualization of calming and soothing scenes to dispel negative thoughts, promoting mental relaxation.

Meaning – Encourages finding purpose or significance in pain or challenging situations, emphasizing the discovery of a silver lining. This aids clients in extracting positivity from every circumstance and facilitates learning.

Prayer – Encompasses seeking strength and confidence through prayer to connect with a spiritual dimension, providing solace and self-assurance.

Relaxation – Focuses on alleviating physical tension and muscle tightness through calming activities such as listening to music, sipping warm milk, or receiving a massage.

One thing in the moment – Promotes mindfulness by directing attention to a neutral, present activity, fostering focus and mental grounding.

Vacation – Suggests taking a mental break from adversity by imagining pleasant scenarios or engaging in enjoyable activities. This could involve visualizing a trip or temporarily disengaging from external pressures.

Encouragement – Involves engaging in positive self-talk to navigate challenging moments, fostering self-support and constructive internal dialogue.

The IMPROVE skill serves the purpose of helping clients tolerate frustration or distress without exacerbating the situation, with the ultimate goal of improvement in ideal conditions. It is particularly beneficial for individuals trapped in seemingly hopeless and uncontrollable situations, where they may experience feelings of hopelessness, hurt, and depression. By applying the IMPROVE skill, individuals in such circumstances can navigate the challenges, regain confidence, and develop a more optimistic perspective.

Mindfulness Skills

So, what precisely does the term "mindfulness" entail? While care scientist Jon Kabat-Zinn provides one definition, for this book, mindfulness is construed as the ability to be cognizant of one's thoughts, emotions, physical sensations, and actions in the present moment, without passing judgment on oneself or the experience.

Perhaps you've encountered expressions like "be in the moment" or "be present." These phrases convey the same idea: to be conscious of what is happening in your immediate experience. However, accomplishing this isn't always a straightforward task. You may be thinking, feeling, sensing, and doing various things simultaneously at any given moment. Consider your current situation – as you read these words, you are likely seated somewhere. Yet, you are also breathing, absorbing the sounds around you, discerning the book's texture, feeling the weight of your body in the chair, and possibly contemplating other thoughts. Furthermore, you may be attuned to your emotional and physical states, such as happiness, sadness, fatigue, or excitement. You might even be aware of bodily sensations, such as your heartbeat or the rhythm of your breath.

Simultaneously, you may be engaged in actions you are unaware of, like tapping your foot, humming, or resting your head in your hand. This breadth of awareness is substantial, and you are presently just engrossed in reading a book. Consider the complexity of your awareness when involved in other aspects of your life, such as conversing with someone or navigating professional interactions. It's acknowledged that nobody can maintain 100 percent awareness continuously. Nevertheless, the more adept you become at cultivating mindfulness, the greater influence you can exert over your life.

However, it's crucial to remember that time is perpetually moving forward, and each passing second brings forth a distinct facet of your life. Given this constant flow, it becomes imperative to cultivate an awareness of "each present moment." Consider, for instance, that as you conclude reading this sentence, the moment you commenced comprehending it has dissipated, and your current experience has transformed. You are now in a different state. The cells within your body are in perpetual flux, continuously renewing and replacing, rendering you physically distinct. Similarly, your thoughts, emotions, sensations, and actions are never precisely replicated in every circumstance; they, too, undergo variations. Hence, developing an awareness of how your experiential landscape evolves in each unique moment of your life becomes paramount.

Moreover, to achieve complete mindfulness of your experiences in the present, it is vital to do so without passing judgment on yourself, your surroundings, or others. In the context of dialectical behavior therapy, this is referred to as radical acceptance. Radical acceptance involves enduring a situation without rendering a judgment or endeavoring to alter it. This principle assumes significance because passing judgment, whether on oneself, one's experience, or another person, distracts from the present moment. For instance, many individuals spend considerable time ruminating on past mistakes or fretting about potential future errors. However, during this contemplation, their focus is no longer on the current moment; their thoughts have drifted elsewhere. Consequently, they dwell in a painful past or an uncertain future, and life takes on a challenging complexion.\

The Importance Of Mindfulness Skills

With a more profound understanding of what mindfulness encompasses—and what it does not—it becomes evident why cultivating this skill holds immense significance. For the purpose of this workbook, let's articulate with precision the reasons driving the imperative need to acquire mindfulness skills. Three pivotal motivations underpin this endeavor:

Enhanced Focus and Emotional Regulation: Mindfulness skills empower you to direct your attention singularly to the present moment, improving your ability to concentrate on one task at a time. This heightened focus contributes to enhanced control over your emotions, aiding in mitigating overwhelming feelings.

Discernment of Judgmental Thoughts: Mindfulness equips you to discern and detach judgmental thoughts from your experiences. These critical thoughts often serve as catalysts for intense and overwhelming emotions. By developing mindfulness, you can identify and separate judgmental tendencies, promoting a more balanced emotional state.

Cultivation of "Wise Mind" in Dialectical Behavior Therapy (DBT):
Mindfulness plays a pivotal role in dialectical behavior therapy, particularly in the cultivation of a skill known as "wise mind." This facet of mindfulness involves accessing a state of balanced and wise decision-making, integrating both rational and emotional aspects. Acquiring mindfulness skills contributes significantly to developing this invaluable aspect of DBT.

A wise mind encapsulates the ability to make sound and healthy decisions regarding your life by integrating both rational thoughts and emotions. This concept recognizes the inherent challenge or near-impossibility of making judicious choices when emotions are intense, irrational, or divergent from what is considered reasonable. Similarly, making informed decisions becomes arduous when thoughts are extreme, illogical, or in conflict with one's emotional state. The essence of a wise mind lies in the harmonious integration of cognitive reasoning and emotional awareness, acknowledging that a balanced amalgamation of these facets is essential for prudent decision-making.

Interpersonal Effectiveness Skills

The significance of relationships cannot be overstated; considering humans are inherently social beings, the importance of interpersonal connections is ingrained. However, maintaining relationships is not without its challenges. Conflicts are inevitable, and as individuals evolve, so do their values and priorities. The acquisition of interpersonal effectiveness skills becomes a crucial tool in constructing and sustaining healthy relationships – mutually beneficial ones, characterized by reciprocal give-and-take, devoid of abuse or exploitation.

Recognizing that relationships extend beyond interactions with others and also encompass our relationship with ourselves, there are three pivotal skill sets within interpersonal effectiveness: FAST, GIVE, and Dear Man.

*FAST Skill*s: These skills revolve around cultivating self-respect, a cornerstone in every relationship. How we carry ourselves profoundly influences the perception others have of us.

GIVE Skills: Focused on our interactions with others, GIVE skills guide how to navigate relationships. This encompasses conflict resolution, care, respect, and validation – essential to fostering healthy connections.

Dear Man Skills: Centered on deriving benefits from relationships, Dear Man skills equip individuals to articulate their needs within a relationship. This includes seeking assistance, asserting boundaries, and negotiating to meet personal requirements.

Maintaining a healthy relationship necessitates a delicate balance among these three skill sets. The key lies in blending these skills judiciously, recognizing that priorities may shift. Sometimes, the focus may be on prioritizing oneself (FAST), while at other times, the emphasis might be on caring for others (GIVE). The skill set Dear Man emphasizes the importance of attending to one's needs within the relationship. Striking a harmonious balance among these skills ensures the dynamic equilibrium required for fostering and sustaining meaningful connections. Therefore, guiding clients to utilize all three skill sets adeptly becomes paramount in pursuing healthy and enduring relationships.

Emotion Regulation Skills

At this stage in the process, we arrive at the penultimate critical skill that is targeted through dialectical behavior therapy techniques - emotional regulation. It's essential to recognize the intricate interconnection among all these skills, each playing a vital role. Mindfulness lays the groundwork by imparting the ability to approach distress tolerance and emotional regulation with the necessary detachment. Distress tolerance, in turn, provides foundational support for managing emotions during particularly challenging times. Emotional regulation, building upon mindfulness and distress tolerance, equips individuals with the tools to regulate their emotions to the utmost extent possible. Interpersonal effectiveness focuses on refining conversational skills in light of the discussed concepts.

Now, delving into emotional regulation, it's essentially a set of procedures and systems designed to assist individuals grappling with difficulties in controlling their emotions consistently and healthily. The core idea revolves around managing harmful emotions in a manner that fosters personal growth and enables more constructive problem-solving. It facilitates cultivating a sense of detachment and acceptance, allowing for a clearer identification of the root causes of problems and devising effective self-help strategies.

The significance of emotional regulation is particularly pronounced for individuals dealing with conditions like borderline personality disorder or those facing emotional instability, including suicidal thoughts. Such individuals often grapple with unpredictable and intense emotions, spanning from anger and depression to anxiety or inexplicable irritation. While these emotions are valid in various situations, the key lies in finding a balance - completely suppressing emotions is as detrimental as experiencing them intensely. The goal is to learn how to feel emotions healthily, preventing them from becoming erratic or irrational. Emotional regulation is a crucial skill, fostering personal development, rational problem-solving, and emotional well-being.

The initial step in mastering emotional regulation involves understanding the emotions at play and the reasons behind their emergence. This can be effectively achieved by employing a technique known as the "story of emotion." This skill is pivotal in dissecting emotions and discerning their precise nature, especially when contending with complex or simultaneous feelings.

Emotions, at times, can be intricate, and it's not uncommon to experience a mix of emotions concurrently, creating a sense of disconnection. When faced with such situations, breaking down the various signals becomes crucial. The multifaceted nature of emotions prompts the need for a nuanced analysis.

The first facet to analyze is the triggering event – what precisely prompted the emotional response. This examination is often revealing, as it sheds light on the specific emotion being experienced. For instance, if someone cuts in front of you in traffic, the emotion of anger might be a valid response.

The second aspect involves scrutinizing how the event was interpreted. Considering one's perspective and assessing how the event was perceived is vital. Returning to analyze the occurrence with a clearer mindset can significantly impact the ensuing emotional reaction.

The third dimension to analyze is the somatic aspect – how the body responds to the emotion. Physical sensations, such as a burning sensation in the stomach or churning sensations, offer valuable insights into the emotional response. This intricate connection between the brain and the body plays a pivotal role in understanding emotions.

Moving on to the fourth aspect, assessing subconscious reactions to the event is imperative. Body language, such as crossed arms, increased emotional guardedness, tense facial expressions, or widened eyes, can indicate different emotions.

The fifth and final consideration is the analysis of the urges associated with the emotion. The inclination to engage in specific actions, such as wanting to retaliate by ramming into the back of someone's car after being cut off, provides a revealing glimpse into the underlying emotion. Recognizing these urges can be key to understanding and managing emotions effectively.

The "story of emotion" technique empowers individuals to break down their emotional experiences by analyzing the triggering event, interpretation, bodily responses, subconscious reactions, and associated urges. This systematic approach facilitates a more nuanced and comprehensive understanding of emotions, laying the groundwork for effective emotional regulation.

The sixth crucial element is the action taken in response to the emotion. Did you resort to cursing or perhaps gesturing angrily, such as flipping someone off? These actions serve as additional indicators of the underlying emotion, offering tangible insights into your feelings.

The last component in the analysis is assigning a name to the emotion, considering all the previously examined factors. If, for instance, your actions and the perceived reason align with anger, acknowledging that you're feeling angry becomes a significant realization.

Despite its apparent simplicity, this process holds substantial importance. Narrating to oneself what emotions are being experienced is a powerful tool for gaining perspective and dissecting the underlying feelings. It acts as a mechanism to recognize irrational emotions, prompting the need for a step back. This recognition is key to effectively moderating and understanding one's emotional state.

The ultimate objective is to distance oneself from the "emotion mind." By achieving this detachment, individuals enhance their capacity to recognize and adapt to situations using conscious and mindful thoughts instead of reacting impulsively based on instinctive and primal impulses.

Turning attention to physical health, practical measures are encapsulated in the acronym PLEASE. The first aspect is Physical health, emphasizing the importance of promptly attending to any illnesses or injuries. Physical well-being directly impacts mental control, and addressing health concerns ensures a stable foundation for emotional regulation.

Moving to the second aspect, Eating habits involves a careful assessment of nutritional intake. Maintaining balanced eating patterns, avoiding extremes, and eating nutritious food contribute significantly to overall well-being. Financial constraints should not be a deterrent, as affordable yet healthy options exist, such as canned vegetables, beans, and rice.

The third aspect highlights the avoidance of drugs. While acknowledging the potential therapeutic benefits of prescribed substances, a cautionary note is sounded against mood-altering substances like alcohol, opiates, and stimulants due to their unpredictable impact on long-term mood and heightened addictive potential.

The fourth element, Sleeping habits, underscores the importance of adequate sleep, aiming for seven to nine hours per night. Disruptions in sleep patterns can significantly impact body chemistry, influencing overall mood.

The fifth and final aspect, Exercise, is lauded as a cornerstone for both mental and physical health. Regular exercise enhances physical appearance and triggers the release of endorphins and other chemicals in the brain, promoting an improved and happier overall mood.

Concluding the PLEASE set, it's essential to complement these measures with cultivating self-discipline. Consistently working on mastering a skill or task daily contributes to a sense of accomplishment and instills valuable lessons in self-discipline and self-control, fostering a heightened sense of competence and well-being.

A fundamental principle within this segment of dialectical behavior therapy involves effectively applying the concept of opposite action. Opposite action is a strategic tool to counteract urges and guide individuals toward doing and feeling what is considered the "right" thing, particularly when confronted with challenging or unjustifiable emotions. By engaging in emotional reflection and detachment, individuals can discern the appropriateness of their emotions, paving the way for the implementation of opposite actions.

Opposite action entails consciously choosing to engage in behavior precisely opposite to the urges associated with a difficult emotion. This technique proves especially valuable when contending with unhealthy and self-destructive emotions like unwarranted anger or annoyance. Instead of succumbing to the impulsive actions dictated by the prevailing emotion, individuals deliberately opt for antithetical actions, effectively steering away from the undesirable emotional state.

This approach facilitates a shift from the unwanted emotion by immersing oneself in the opposite emotion. While it may initially appear simplistic, the intuitive nature of this technique often proves remarkably effective, offering significant emotional relief in volatile situations.

Now, if the emotion experienced is justified, the skill of problem-solving comes into play. Detaching oneself from the situation, individuals can objectively assess the circumstances and determine actionable steps to address the problem. If there's a viable solution, taking reasonable and effective measures to alleviate the situation is recommended. However, acceptance becomes key if the situation is beyond one's control. Acknowledging the reality and allowing oneself to feel the emotion without futile resistance becomes crucial to emotional regulation.

The final key concept aligns closely with the themes of acceptance and mindfulness. It involves the practice of letting go of emotions. Contrary to suppressing emotions entirely, the aim is to experience them rationally and relatively healthily. Deliberate contemplation of the prevailing emotion and genuine acknowledgment form the basis of acceptance. In this context, acceptance does not mandate an immediate reaction; rather, it signifies a conscious awareness that the emotion is present. Once acknowledged, individuals can allow the emotion to pass over them, fostering a sense of emotional balance and well-being.

SECTION FOUR: STRESS AND SOCIAL ANXIETY MANAGEMENT

Origins and Historical Evolution: The term "stress" traces its roots to the Latin "strictus," signifying "tight" or "compressed." In the 17th century, among the Anglo-Saxons, stress conveyed "difficulty" and "affliction." It wasn't until subsequent centuries, particularly in metallurgy, that stress came to represent a force — the pressure exerted on an object to test its resistance.

A pivotal shift occurred between 1910 and 1920 when biologist Walter Cannon introduced stress as a concept denoting the body's alarm reaction to external stimuli. However, it was Hans Selye, a Canadian physician of Austrian origin, who, in the 1930s, opened a significant chapter on the effects of external stimuli (stressors) on organisms, a subject still under study today.

Experiments involving laboratory animals subjected to severe administration of harmful substances revealed a syndrome characterized by adrenal gland cortex hypertrophy, thymus and lymphatic gland atrophy, and recurrent gastric ulcers. Selye identified this as a fundamental biological response, independent of the stressor type, involving the activation of two endocrine glands — the pituitary and current. This complex of symptoms and biological changes was encapsulated in the "general adaptation syndrome."

As Selye concluded, stress is the organism's adaptation to changes in internal homeostasis induced by stressors. He outlined the stress response in three stages:

1. Alarm Phase: Activation of the hypothalamus-pituitary-cortico-surrene axis and the adrenal medulla, releasing cortisol, adrenaline, and noradrenaline, mobilizing the body's defenses.
2. Resistance Phase: Continued overproduction of cortisol with consequences, primarily the suppression of immune defenses, as stress persists.
3. Exhaustion Phase: Culminating in adrenal gland exhaustion and the death of experimental animals, often exhibiting gastric mucosa ulceration due to increased acidity from hypersecretion secondary to hypercortisolemia.

Evolution of Stress Understanding: Numerous scientific studies have demonstrated that mice and humans activate the same fundamental stress response when confronted with various stimuli, such as a virus, threat, intense emotion, or environmental factors. Contrary to the prevailing negative connotation associated with stress, physiological reactions are crucial in enhancing the organism's response to a stressful event, promoting adaptation. However, prolonged exposure to stress becomes potentially harmful and can lead to pathology. This necessitates an exploration of stress physiology and an analysis of emotions.

The stress axis is the focal point for neuroendocrine circuits, acting as a vital junction in regulating the organism's physiology. It consists of two arms: a chemical arm and a nervous arm. The chemical arm originates from the hypothalamus, releasing corticotropin-releasing hormone (CRH) and arginine-vasopressin (AVP), stimulating the pituitary gland to produce adrenocorticotropic hormone (ACTH). ACTH, in turn, reaches the adrenal cortex, prompting the production of steroid hormones, primarily cortisol. Cortisol, with its circadian rhythm, exerts a metabolic influence, enhancing blood sugar levels, lipid and cholesterol rates, bone structure reabsorption, gastric acidity, and anti-inflammatory and anti-allergic actions, among others. Excess cortisol secretion can adversely affect metabolism, bones, brain, immunity, blood, and circulation.

The nervous arm involves the sympathetic nervous system and the "locus coeruleus" nuclei in the hypothalamus, which stimulates the adrenal medulla to release catecholamines (adrenaline, noradrenaline, and dopamine). This brain-adrenal connection induces physiological responses, such as increased heart rate, shortened breath, muscle contraction, and icy sweating during stress. The interplay between chemical and nervous mechanisms, along with feedback control mechanisms, regulates the stress response. Additionally, stimuli, both physical (intense activity, trauma, pain, fever) and psychological, can modulate ACTH and cortisol levels. In synergy with catecholamines, other hormones come into play when the body is required to sustain a state of maximum alertness for an extended duration due to persistent stress.

The Effects Of Stress You Must Know

In the intricate tapestry of our lives, stress is a common thread that weaves through various experiences. Understanding the effects of stress is paramount for navigating its complexities and safeguarding our well-being. This composition aims to unravel the layers of stress, offering essential insights into its profound effects that everyone must know.

Physiological Ramifications: Stress triggers a cascade of physiological responses designed to prepare us for challenges. While short-term stress can enhance performance, chronic stress takes a toll on our bodies. The prolonged release of stress hormones, including cortisol and adrenaline, contributes to disrupted sleep, weakened immune function, and an increased susceptibility to health issues like cardiovascular diseases.

Cognitive Challenges: The cognitive impact of stress is profound. Chronic stress has been linked to cognitive impairments such as memory lapses, difficulties in concentration, and impaired decision-making. The overwhelming demands of a stress-laden lifestyle can overwhelm our cognitive capacities, affecting our ability to think clearly and solve problems effectively.

Emotional Turmoil: Stress is intricately intertwined with our emotional well-being. Feelings of anxiety, irritability, and mood swings become pervasive, affecting personal relationships and overall life satisfaction. Long-term exposure to stress can contribute to the development or exacerbation of mental health disorders, emphasizing the crucial connection between stress management and emotional resilience.

Interpersonal Strain: Stress reverberates through our relationships, causing strains and fractures. Communication breakdowns, increased conflicts, and a diminished capacity for empathy can erode connections with loved ones. Recognizing the impact of stress on relationships underscores the importance of cultivating effective coping mechanisms for individuals and fostering supportive environments.

Professional Implications: In the workplace, stress is an omnipresent factor that can significantly impact professional dynamics. Intense workloads, tight deadlines, and job uncertainty create a stressful environment. The consequences range from decreased productivity to burnout, highlighting the need for proactive stress management strategies to maintain a healthy work-life balance.

Behavioral Changes and Coping Mechanisms: Individuals under stress often resort to behavioral changes as coping mechanisms. While some adopt healthy strategies such as exercise and mindfulness, others may engage in maladaptive behaviors like overeating or substance abuse. Recognizing and choosing effective coping mechanisms is pivotal in mitigating the adverse effects of stress on behavior.

The Most Effective Ways To Handle Stress Productively

Mindfulness and Relaxation Techniques: Cultivating mindfulness through practices like meditation, deep breathing, or yoga can be instrumental in stress management. These techniques help individuals stay grounded in the present moment, reducing the impact of overwhelming thoughts and emotions. Regular practice enhances self-awareness and fosters a calmer, more centered state of mind.

Time Management and Prioritization: Effectively managing time and setting priorities are essential tools in combating stress. Breaking down tasks into manageable components, setting realistic deadlines, and learning to delegate can prevent feeling overwhelmed. This strategic approach empowers individuals to navigate challenges systematically, reducing stress associated with looming deadlines.

Social Support Networks: Strengthening social connections is a powerful buffer against stress. Sharing concerns, seeking advice, or spending quality time with friends and family can provide emotional support. A robust social support network alleviates stress and provides a sense of belonging and security during challenging times.

Regular Exercise: Physical activity is a natural stress reliever. Regular exercise releases endorphins, the body's natural mood elevators, promoting a sense of well-being. Whether it's a brisk walk, a workout session, or a recreational activity, incorporating exercise into one's routine is a proactive way to manage stress and enhance overall health.

Healthy Lifestyle Choices: Adopting a healthy lifestyle contributes significantly to stress reduction. Adequate sleep, a balanced diet, and hydration play pivotal roles in maintaining physical and mental well-being. Nourishing the body with proper nutrition and rest creates a foundation for resilience in the face of stressors.

Effective Communication: Clear and open communication is key to managing stress in interpersonal relationships. Expressing thoughts and feelings assertively while actively listening to others fosters understanding and prevents misunderstandings that can lead to stress. Developing strong communication skills enhances relationship dynamics and reduces unnecessary tension.

Professional Boundaries: Establishing and maintaining clear boundaries in the professional sphere is essential for managing stress at work. Learning to say no when necessary, setting realistic expectations, and recognizing the importance of breaks contribute to a healthier work environment. Effective professional boundaries prevent burnout and improve overall job satisfaction.

Therapeutic Interventions: Seeking professional help through therapy or counseling can provide valuable insights and coping strategies for managing stress. Therapists can assist individuals in understanding the root causes of stress, developing resilience, and implementing effective coping mechanisms tailored to their specific needs.

Relaxation Exercises To Calm Your Emotions

1. Box Breathing:

- *Sit Comfortably*: Find a quiet place to sit or lie down. Sit comfortably with your back straight.

- *Inhale (Count of 4):* Inhale quietly through your nose to the count of four. Feel the air filling your lungs.

- *Hold Breath (Count of 4)*: Hold your breath for a count of four. Keep your lungs filled with air.

- *Exhale (Count of 4):* Exhale slowly and completely through your mouth to the count of four. Empty your lungs.

- *Hold Breath (Count of 4):* Hold your breath again for a count of four before beginning the next cycle.

- Repeat: Continue this cycle for several minutes. Focus on the rhythmic pattern and let other thoughts drift away.

2. Body Scan Meditation:

- *Get in a Comfortable Position:* Find a quiet, comfortable space. Sit or lie down with your eyes closed.

- *Focus on Breathing:* Take a few deep breaths to relax. Focus your attention on your breath to bring awareness to the present moment.

- *Start with Your Toes:* Bring attention to your toes. Notice any sensations, tension, or relaxation. Breathe into any tension, then release.

- *Move to Feet, Ankles, and Upwards:* Gradually move your focus through each part of your body, paying attention to sensations. Ankles, calves, knees, thighs, and so on.

- *Breathe into Tension:* If you find tension, breathe into that area. Imagine sending your breath to that specific spot.

- *Continue Upwards:* Work your way up through your abdomen, chest, shoulders, arms, and hands. Take your time with each area.

- *Focus on the Neck and Head*: Pay special attention to your neck and head. Release any tension. Let your jaw relax, and feel the sensations in your face.

- *Scan Your Entire Body*: Once you've reached the top of your head, scan your entire body as a whole. Feel the connection between your body and the surface it's resting on.

- *Open Your Eyes*: When you're ready, open your eyes slowly. Take a moment to reorient yourself.

2. Focused Attention Meditation:

- *Choose a Point of Focus*: Sit comfortably and choose a point of focus. This can be your breath, a candle flame, or a specific thought.

- *Breathe Naturally:* Allow your breath to be natural. Don't try to control it; simply observe.

- *Redirect Your Mind:* If your mind starts to wander (which is normal), gently bring it back to your chosen point of focus.

- Be Present: Stay present in the moment. Notice sensations, thoughts, and feelings without judgment.

- *Start with Short Sessions:* If you're new to meditation, start with short sessions and gradually increase the duration as you become more comfortable.

- *Practice Regularly*: Consistency is key. Practice this focused attention regularly to train your mind to stay present.

3. Yoga:

- *Choose a Quiet Space:* Find a quiet and comfortable space where you won't be disturbed.

- *Get Yoga Attire:* Wear comfortable clothing that allows for easy movement.

- *Select a Yoga Mat:* If you have one, lay out a yoga mat to provide a clean and supportive surface.

- *Start with Warm-Up Poses:* Begin with gentle warm-up poses to prepare your body. This could include neck rolls, shoulder stretches, and gentle twists.

- *Follow a Routine or Video:* You can follow a specific yoga routine or use online videos. Poses like Downward Dog, Child's Pose, and Warrior Poses are commonly practiced.

- *Focus on Breathing:* Pay attention to your breath. Inhale deeply and exhale slowly, syncing your breath with your movements.

- *End with Relaxation Poses:* Finish your session with relaxation poses like Savasana, allowing your body to relax fully.

- *Stay Hydrated:* Keep water nearby to stay hydrated throughout your practice.

4. Tai Chi:

- *Find a Quiet Outdoor or Indoor Space:* Tai Chi is often practiced outdoors, but you can also adapt it to indoor spaces.

- *Wear Comfortable Clothing*: Choose loose and comfortable clothing for unrestricted movement.

- *Begin with Deep Breaths:* Stand with feet shoulder-width apart. Inhale deeply through your nose, allowing your abdomen to expand, and exhale through your mouth, releasing tension.

- *Learn Basic Tai Chi Movements:* Tai Chi consists of slow, flowing movements. Start with basic movements like "Grasp the Sparrow's Tail" or "Waving Hands Like Clouds."

- *Focus on Relaxation:* Emphasize relaxation in your movements. Tai Chi is about harmonizing the body and mind.

- *Maintain Proper Posture*: Pay attention to your posture. Keep your back straight, shoulders relaxed, and knees slightly bent.

- *Flow from One Movement to Another*: Tai Chi is a continuous flow of movements. Transition smoothly from one posture to the next.

- *Practice Regularly*: Consistency is important. Aim for regular practice to experience the full benefits.

5. Aromatherapy:

- *Gather Essential Oils*: Choose essential oils known for relaxation, such as lavender, chamomile, or eucalyptus.

- *Select a Diffuser:* Use an aromatherapy diffuser to disperse the essential oils into the air.

- *Add Water and Oils:* Follow the diffuser instructions, usually involving adding water and a few drops of your chosen essential oil.

- *Place in a Relaxing Space:* Put the diffuser in a quiet, calming space.

- *Turn On the Diffuser:* Activate the diffuser to release the aromatic mist into the air.

- *Breathe Deeply*: Inhale the soothing aroma deeply. Focus on the scents and let them promote relaxation.

- *Combine with Other Relaxation Activities:* Use aromatherapy with meditation, yoga, or other relaxation techniques for enhanced effects.

- *Experiment with Blends:* Explore different essential oil blends to find what works best for you. Adjust the intensity by adding more or fewer drops of oil.

6. Grounding Techniques:

- *Find a Comfortable Position:* Sit or stand comfortably, feeling the connection between your body and the ground.

- *Focus on Breathing*: Take deep breaths, inhaling slowly through your nose and exhaling through your mouth.

- *Engage Your Senses:* Identify and name five things you can see, four things you can touch, three things you can hear, two things you can smell, and one thing you can taste.

- *Use Physical Objects*: Hold a small, comforting object in your hands, feeling its texture and weight. Concentrate on the sensations it provides.

- *Stamp Your Feet*: If sitting, stamp your feet on the ground gently. Feel the rhythmic impact and focus on the sensation.

- *Count Backwards*: Count backward from 100 by sevens or threes, engaging your mind in a task to redirect your thoughts.

- *Recite Affirmations*: Repeat positive affirmations to yourself, reinforcing a sense of safety and control.

- *Grounding with Ice*: Hold an ice cube in your hand and feel its coldness, bringing your attention to the present moment.

7. Listening to Calming Music:

- *Create a Playlist*: Compile a playlist of calming music. Choose tracks with soothing melodies or sounds of nature.

- *Find a Quiet Space*: Pick a quiet environment to fully immerse yourself in the music.

- *Use Headphones:* For a more immersive experience, use headphones to eliminate external distractions.

- *Close Your Eyes:* Sit or lie down comfortably. Close your eyes to enhance your focus on the auditory experience.

- *Focus on the Music:* Pay attention to the details of the music – the instruments, rhythms, and overall composition.

- *Breathe in Sync*: Align your breath with the music. Inhale deeply during calm passages and exhale during softer moments.

- *Let Your Mind Wander:* Allow your mind to drift with the music, letting go of stressors and embracing the present moment.

- *Repeat as Needed:* Use calming music as a tool to unwind whenever you feel stressed or overwhelmed.

8. Journaling:

- *Set Aside Time:* Allocate a specific time for journaling where you won't be rushed.

- *Choose a Comfortable Space:* Sit in a comfortable, quiet space conducive to introspection.

-

- *Pick Your Journal*: Select a journal or notebook for your thoughts and reflections.

- *Start with Prompts:* If unsure where to begin, use prompts like "Today, I feel..." or "Things on my mind..."

- *Write Freely:* Allow your thoughts to flow freely onto the paper. Don't worry about grammar or structure.

- *Express Emotions*: Describe your emotions and experiences without judgment. Be honest with yourself.

- *Reflect on Solutions:* If you're dealing with challenges, reflect on potential solutions or coping strategies.

- *End with Gratitude*: Conclude your journaling session by noting a few things you're grateful for, fostering a positive mindset.

9. Mindful Walking:

- *Choose a Walking Path*: Find a quiet and safe outdoor space for walking.

- *Stand Mindfully:* Begin by standing still and taking a few deep breaths. Center yourself in the present moment.

- *Start Walking Slowly*: Initiate slow, deliberate steps. Feel the sensations in your feet as they connect with the ground.

- *Focus on Your Steps:* Direct your attention to the act of walking. Notice how your body moves with each step.

- *Engage Your Senses:* Pay attention to the sights, sounds, and smells around you. Fully immerse yourself in the experience.

- *Mindful Breathing:* Coordinate your breath with your steps. Inhale and exhale rhythmically.

- *Release Tension:* If you feel tension, consciously release it with each exhale. Allow your body to relax.

- *Practice Gratitude:* Express gratitude for the ability to walk and the beauty of your surroundings.

Social Anxiety

There exist numerous factors contributing to anxiety, and the available treatments vary based on the severity of the disorder. Opting for consultation with a doctor or therapist proves to be the optimal approach. Professionals in these fields tailor a comprehensive treatment plan encompassing medication, meditation, self-care techniques, breathing exercises, and more. This personalized approach considers the individual's anxiety level, recommending appropriate interventions. Meditation consistently features as a component in the treatment spectrum across different anxiety degrees.

It is crucial to understand that meditation doesn't serve as a standalone treatment for anxiety but operates as a complementary method, offering benefits that surpass documented scientific evidence. Through meditation, individuals learn to focus on sensations mindfully, discerning what they can control and what lies beyond their influence. This book particularly caters to those not necessarily dealing with chronic anxiety but facing persistent worries or daily stress, providing insights into self-care.

Within these pages, readers gain insights into the nature of anxiety and its triggers. More importantly, the book delves into the role of meditation in alleviating anxiety, presenting brief yet effective meditation practices. The ultimate goal is to empower individuals to infuse tranquility and serenity into their lives. Left untreated, anxiety can escalate, significantly impacting various facets of a person's life. What may start as a seemingly minor concern can evolve into chronic anxiety, disrupting emotional and mental well-being in day-to-day living.

Understanding Anxiety:

"I'm struggling to breathe!"
"My heart is racing uncontrollably!"
"Why are my legs trembling?"
"I feel nauseous and sick to my stomach."
"I need a drink or my pills to calm this anxious heart. I can't bear it."
"Why does it feel like the world is crashing down on me?"

If you've ever found yourself echoing these sentiments, you might be familiar with these symptoms – it could be anxiety or perhaps even a panic disorder. Anxiety, a natural human response to stress, manifests as a sense of fear or nervousness about anticipated events. This emotional state is not limited to major life events such as exams, childbirth, or job interviews. Still, it can also stem from everyday challenges like financial woes, health concerns, or work-related stress. Additionally, anxiety can surface in response to specific fears like needles, flying, or encounters with wildlife.

While the triggers for anxiety vary among individuals, experiencing anxiety at some point in life is a universal phenomenon.

In the early stages of human existence, the body developed alarm systems in response to incoming dangers or the presence of predators. These alarms manifested as heightened heartbeat, increased perspiration, and heightened awareness or sensitivity. An adrenaline rush would signal the brain, initiating reactions commonly known as the 'fight-or-flight' response. This mechanism allowed individuals to confront or evade threats and crises swiftly.

While escaping predators is less of a concern today, anxieties have evolved and primarily revolve around modern-day issues like work, health, finances, and family, often without necessitating a 'fight-or-flight' reaction. The fear and apprehension before a significant event or challenging situation echo the original survival response, still relevant today. For instance, fearing a lightning strike prompts an instinctive avoidance of open fields during thunderstorms.

Stress, fear, and anxiety are universal feelings, yet they differ from anxiety disorders. If intense anxiety persists for more than six months and significantly disrupts daily routines, it could indicate an anxiety disorder. Anxiety-related disorders are categorized into three main groups: 1) anxiety disorders, 2) obsessive-compulsive and related disorders, and 3) trauma-related disorders. Worry or distress persists in these disorders, intensifying over time and impacting daily activities and relationships.

Identifying the cause of anxiety and assessing whether symptom severity is proportionate to the cause can help determine if one is dealing with an anxiety disorder. Individuals with an anxiety disorder may react as if in real danger even when there is none. Diagnosing anxiety disorders can be challenging, making it advisable to consult licensed professionals such as psychologists or psychiatrists for accurate assessments and diagnoses.

Common Types Of Anxiety Disorder

Diverse anxiety disorders encapsulate a spectrum of mental health conditions, each distinguished by unique characteristics and manifestations:

Generalized Anxiety Disorder (GAD): This disorder is typified by persistent and excessive worry about various facets of life, often without a specific triggering event. Individuals with GAD may find it challenging to control their anxious thoughts, leading to heightened stress levels impacting daily functioning.

Social Anxiety Disorder: People grappling with social anxiety experience intense fear and apprehension in social settings. This anxiety may be rooted in the anticipation of negative judgments from others, leading to avoidance of social interactions and hindering the formation of meaningful relationships.

Panic Disorder: Characterized by recurrent and unexpected panic attacks, panic disorder brings about intense episodes of fear accompanied by physical symptoms like rapid heartbeat, shortness of breath, and a sense of impending doom. Persistent worry about the recurrence of these attacks further characterizes this disorder.

Agoraphobia: Agoraphobia is marked by an intense fear of situations perceived as difficult to escape or where help may not be readily available. Individuals with agoraphobia often avoid crowded places or situations that trigger distress, limiting their daily activities.

Specific Phobias: Specific phobias involve an irrational and overwhelming fear of particular objects, situations, or activities. These fears range from common stimuli like heights, animals, or flying to more unusual or specific triggers. Individuals may go to great lengths to avoid encountering their feared stimuli.

Understanding these classifications is pivotal for mental health professionals in diagnosing and tailoring effective treatment plans for individuals experiencing these anxiety disorders. Treatment may involve therapeutic interventions, medication, or a combination of both, depending on the severity and specific symptoms of the disorder.

Effective Coping Skills For Anxiety

Mindfulness Meditation: Engage in mindfulness practices, focusing on the present moment without judgment. Techniques like deep breathing and guided meditation can help calm the mind.

Regular Exercise: Incorporate regular physical activity into your routine. Exercise is known to release endorphins, which can alleviate stress and anxiety.

Healthy Lifestyle Choices: Prioritize a balanced diet, adequate sleep, and hydration. A well-nourished and rested body contributes to better emotional well-being.

Limit Caffeine and Sugar Intake: High caffeine and sugar consumption can exacerbate anxiety. Consider reducing these stimulants in your diet.

Breathing Exercises: Practice deep breathing exercises to activate the body's relaxation response. Techniques like diaphragmatic breathing can help regulate stress levels.

Establish a Routine: Create a structured daily routine. Predictability can provide a sense of control and stability, reducing anxiety.

Social Connections: Maintain supportive relationships. Sharing your feelings with trusted friends or family can offer emotional support and understanding.

Limit Exposure to Stressors: Identify and minimize exposure to stressors when possible. Create a conducive environment for relaxation and well-being.

Professional Counseling: Seek guidance from mental health professionals. Therapy sessions like cognitive-behavioral therapy (CBT) can provide coping mechanisms and tools.

Set Realistic Goals: Break down tasks into manageable goals. Setting realistic objectives helps prevent feeling overwhelmed, reducing anxiety.

Journaling: Write down your thoughts and feelings in a journal. This practice can provide clarity, allowing you to understand better and manage your emotions.

Mindful Walking: Take mindful walks, paying attention to your surroundings. This combines physical activity with mindfulness, promoting relaxation.

Hobbies and Leisure Activities: Engage in activities you enjoy. Hobbies and leisure pursuits provide a healthy distraction and contribute to overall well-being.

Limit Information Overload: Reduce exposure to distressing news or information. Constant exposure to negative stimuli can heighten anxiety levels.

Progressive Muscle Relaxation: Practice progressive muscle relaxation to release tension in the body. This involves systematically tensing and then relaxing different muscle groups.

Remember that coping strategies can vary from person to person. Experimenting with different techniques to identify what works best for you may be beneficial. If anxiety persists or worsens, seeking professional help is crucial for personalized guidance and support.

SECTION FIVE: ANGER COPING MECHANISMS

Anger is a powerful and natural emotion everyone experiences at various times. While anger itself is not inherently negative, the way we manage and express it can significantly impact our well-being and relationships.

Understanding and employing effective anger coping mechanisms is essential for maintaining emotional balance and fostering healthier connections with others. In this exploration, we delve into practical strategies and techniques designed to help individuals constructively navigate and channel their anger. Discovering constructive ways to cope with anger is not only a personal growth journey but also a crucial element in building resilient and harmonious relationships.

1. How To Use Mindfulness Skills To Manage Anger

Effectively managing intense anger issues can be likened to navigating through a dark room, desperately searching for an exit. In such a scenario, a flashlight becomes an indispensable tool, and in anger management, awareness serves as that guiding light. Knowledge emerges as a crucial instrument in gaining control over anger:

Anticipation and Deterrence: Mindfulness acts as an early warning system, enabling you to foresee and prevent angry outbursts. By paying attention to the signs and consequences of anger and recognizing its triggers, you can intercept it before things escalate.

Control and Endurance: Mindfulness empowers you to manage and endure through moments of rage. By closely observing the anger's ebb and flow, you understand that frustration is transient, that detrimental outcomes aren't inevitable, and that you can navigate through the emotion without succumbing to it.

Avoidance of Aggravation: Mindfulness aids in steering clear of activities that exacerbate anger, such as obsessive rumination, preventing the escalation of the emotional wave.

Freedom and Mastery: Cultivating mindfulness provides a sense of freedom and mastery over anger. By exercising vigilance without necessarily acting on the anger, you transition from a position of powerlessness, akin to a swimmer engulfed by the anger wave, to adeptly riding the wave like a seasoned surfer.

Release from Attachment: Mindfulness enables you to relinquish attachments to specific outcomes or the compulsion for things to be different. Many individuals experience distress because they cling to the need for alternative circumstances, people, thoughts, feelings, or even a different version of themselves. Rather than futilely grasping at an alternative reality, mindfulness encourages accepting the present situation.

Applying Mindfulness To Your Experiences

Mindfulness entails focusing on something while relinquishing biases and preconceptions, contemplating and recollecting. To truly attend to something, one must step back mentally and observe it objectively, refraining from labeling it as good or bad, right or wrong. Instead of attempting to manipulate the situation, embrace the experience without judgment, irrespective of personal preferences. This approach mirrors stepping outside in the morning, observing the weather—be it the warmth of the sun, the clouds in the sky, or the sensation of rain—without attaching undue significance. When confronted with frustration or anger, responding mindfully proves more effective than reactive behavior.

Begin by honing the skill of observing your everyday encounters with diligence, and gradually applying these techniques to instances of frustration.

Before delving into the exercises, it's crucial to remember a key tip. While concentrating on one thing, your attention is prone to shift. Minds naturally engage in thinking, planning, stressing, meditating, daydreaming, and fantasizing, diverting focus from the intended subject. The essence of attentive observation is not about rigidly adhering to a singular focus; rather, it involves gently guiding your thoughts back to the focal point whenever distractions arise. For instance, if you're attending to morning birds and trees but are entangled in afternoon to-do lists, redirect your focus to the avian melodies and foliage.

Attending to one thing at a time poses challenges akin to weightlifting, where the mindfulness muscles improve with consistent practice. The exercises provided below serve as a starting point for cultivating the skill of mindfully observing your experiences. Regular practice can not only introduce you to the basics of mindfulness but may also enable you to extend this mindful awareness to various aspects of your daily life. Consequently, heightened awareness and attentiveness to each moment may lead to stress reduction and a richer engagement with life.

Prepare a cup of your preferred hot beverage—coffee, tea, warm milk—and once it reaches a comfortable temperature, cup your hands around the mug. Focus on the warmth and any aromas emanating from the drink. As you slowly lift the cup to your lips, take note of the steam and warmth on your nose and face. Sip the beverage slowly, paying attention to the liquid's sensation in your mouth, identifying any tastes that arise, and observing the swallowing process.

Find a serene spot outdoors, whether in your backyard, on the porch, or in a nearby park with visible trees. Observe the birds as they gracefully move from branch to branch and tree to tree. Pay attention to their movements, shapes, sizes, colors, and the melodic sounds of their chirping.

Embark on a mindful walk, focusing on the sensations beneath your feet. Regardless of discomfort, anchor your attention to the feelings, including pressure, temperature, and strain. Mindfully attend to these sensations without attempting to modify or alter them unless there's an injury.

Knowing Your Early Anger Signs

After consistently practicing mindful attention to your anger, you'll gain familiarity with the emotions that accompany it. This is crucial because anger can sneak up on you, often more unexpectedly than other emotions. Have you ever experienced an explosive outburst without apparent warning or reacted more intensely than the situation warranted? Consider returning home from work, and feeling incredibly upset about someone's actions. Recognizing the early signs of frustration and milder forms of anger throughout the day could have enabled you to address and manage your anger before arriving home.

Engaging in detective work may reveal the early signs of building frustration. Reflecting on your day, you might recall mild anger triggered by seemingly trivial annoyances. Early signs of anger can manifest as subtle physiological changes like mild muscle tension, negative emotions involving persistent negative thoughts, or behavioral patterns such as increased agitation.

Identifying these early signs provides an opportunity for proactive intervention to prevent an explosive reaction. For instance, if you sense stress accumulating at work, consider implementing techniques from this guide, such as self-soothing, distraction, or reversing behavior. Alternatively, suppose you notice telltale signs of escalating frustration during a home dinner. In that case, you can take proactive steps to effectively address and manage your anger.

Getting Along the Wave of Your Anger

A potent method for incorporating anger management techniques into your daily life involves consciously navigating the wave of frustration. The next time you find yourself angered, irritated, or annoyed, take a mental step back and direct your attention to how your body responds. Identify where the sensations of anger are most palpable without passing judgment, attempting to alter or eradicate them. Engage with your emotions without succumbing to immediate action, recognizing that emotions, much like waves, rise and fall swiftly, provided you refrain from retriggering them, such as dwelling in an anger-inducing environment or persistent rumination.

Allow the wave of anger to rise and subside without yielding to impulsive reactions. Envision yourself as a surfer skillfully navigating the wave of wrath toward the shore. It's crucial to exercise caution in your initial responses when beginning to navigate your anger. In situations that provoke anger, the initial instinct might be to act swiftly, but abstaining from immediate action is often beneficial. If engaged in a conversation, abruptly halting might seem peculiar, but taking a brief pause to let the anger subside before responding can be productive. As you ride out the wave of anger, the subsequent step involves employing a technique that facilitates one of three objectives:

A. Refraining from actions exacerbating the situation.

B. Effectively communicating with those involved, or

C. Temporarily withdrawing from the scenario until a return with a more composed and thoughtful demeanor is possible.

2. How To Use Opposite Action To Reduce Anger

A highly effective emotional regulation skill employed in Dialectical Behavior Therapy (DBT) is known as 'opposite action.' The concept behind opposite action is straightforward – it entails engaging in actions contrary to what you are feeling or acting against your instinctual response. This technique proves beneficial when grappling with emotions that seem disproportionate to the situation's reality. It's important to acknowledge the validity of your emotions, but the intensity may not align with the circumstances. Additionally, the opposite action can be applied when you are confronted with urges and are tempted to act upon them, recognizing that succumbing to such impulses would be ineffective.

For instance, if you are experiencing intense anger and have the urge to engage in physical confrontation, the opposite action would involve refraining from a fight and choosing to walk away from the situation. It's crucial to note that the opposite action doesn't entail suppressing or invalidating your emotions; you will still experience them, but your actions will deliberately counter them. Over time, consistently practicing the opposite action can transform your emotional responses, leading to more favorable outcomes. For example, responding to anxiety that inhibits you from leaving the house involves facing your fears and stepping outside. This may initially be challenging, but with each accomplishment, it becomes progressively easier until the fear diminishes.

In the context of depression, where the inclination might be to remain in bed, avoid social interactions, and abstain from activities, the opposite action involves engaging in energetic pursuits like running, going to the gym, or participating in a vigorous workout. While the initial effort might be challenging, breaking the inertia can alleviate depressive feelings. Physical activity stimulates the release of dopamine and serotonin in the brain, contributing to an improved mood. Even a simple walk can be a step toward overcoming the inertia associated with depression and experiencing a positive shift in emotional well-being.

When grappling with sadness, the conventional response might involve shedding tears as a means of emotional release. However, employing the opposite action in this scenario entails doing something that evokes laughter. While there are instances when allowing oneself to cry can be therapeutic, persistent and constant crying may warrant a shift in approach. By opting for the opposite action of laughter, you acknowledge and express your emotions differently, steering the outcome toward a positive trajectory. This approach encourages a constructive engagement with emotions, offering a distinct and uplifting perspective amid moments of sadness.

The Easiest Ways To Implementing Opposite Actions

Implementing the opposite action involves a systematic approach that begins with identifying the emotions at play. Suppose, for instance, you are grappling with anxiety before a test. The initial step entails scrutinizing the factual basis of your anxiety. Assess the evidence, reminding yourself that you have studied, acknowledge your satisfactory performance in previous tests, and recognize that it is not a midterm or unit test. By confronting the facts, you may realize that your level of anxiety may not align with the situation's reality.

The subsequent step involves identifying your urges, including thoughts of skipping school, feigning illness, or attempting to reschedule the test by informing your professor. However, upon closer examination, you discern these urges are unlikely to be effective solutions. While they may provide temporary relief by postponing the test, they could exacerbate anxiety in the long run.

The third step in employing the opposite action is to consult your wise mind, a fusion of emotions and logical reasoning. In the context of test anxiety, the opposite action becomes clear – proceed to take the test. Engage your wise mind by contemplating the most effective course of action in the given circumstance. This might involve attending school, discussing your concerns with your professor, seeking guidance from a counselor, or taking any action conducive to long-term anxiety reduction.

Having identified the opposite actions and determined the most suitable course, it is imperative to act on it decisively. Attend school and take the test, contrary to the initial urges or impulses. By reinforcing the notion that taking the test is the right action, your brain begins to adapt. Post-test, communicate with your teacher about your anxiety, expressing a desire to address concerns for future assessments. Request additional support or resources, demonstrating a commitment to managing anxiety more effectively. If the first attempt at the opposite action does not yield the desired outcome, return to your wise mind, reassess, and persist with acting oppositely until you discover the approach that resonates with you.

The opposite action technique is precious when the intensity of the emotion being experienced does not align with the factual circumstances or when an emotion persists for an extended period beyond its typical duration.

To implement the opposite action effectively, the initial step is to identify the specific emotions you aim to modify. Subsequently, assess whether the emotions being exhibited correspond with the facts of the situation. If the emotion is incongruent with the factual context, proceed to identify the associated action urges. For example, if the emotion is anger and does not fit the situation's facts, the action urges might include screaming, yelling, throwing things, or raising your voice.

Following the identification of both the emotion and its associated action urges, the key is to engage in the opposite action actively. Consistently and repetitively perform actions contrary to the emotional impulses and action urges. This ongoing practice diminishes the inclination to act on the urges and reduces emotional sensitivity.

Persistence is crucial in the application of the opposite action. Continue practicing the opposite action until the frequency of succumbing to action urges diminishes and emotional reactivity decreases. Through repetitive and dedicated practice, you condition yourself to respond more effectively to the identified emotions. The following outlines the opposite actions suitable for various emotions:

Angry mood: When your anger appears disproportionate to the actual situation, the recommended opposite action is to avoid rather than launch an attack on the individual causing your anger. It's important to note that gentle, not complete, avoidance is advised. If you find yourself on the verge of yelling or shouting at the person, stepping away is recommended until you've regained your composure. Engage in paced breathing during this time-out, and when you feel sufficiently calmer, you can return to the person. Individuals with Borderline Personality Disorder (BPD) often experience intense reactions to anger, and taking a moment for slow, deep breaths can be an effective strategy to regain composure before attempting to resume communication.

Fearful mood: When fear seems disproportionate to the actual situation, the recommended opposite action is repeatedly confronting what you're afraid of. For example, if you're apprehensive about attending your exposure group, the most effective approach is to attend the group repeatedly. Additionally, facing people, activities, tasks, or events that evoke fear and practicing engagement can help foster a sense of control and confidence over these fears. Maintaining focused sight and hearing during the opposite action for fear is crucial, reminding yourself that you are physically and mentally safe despite the fear. While engaging in fear-based opposite action, consider adjusting your posture to exude confidence, maintain a confident tone of voice, practice paced breathing, and deliberately breathe slowly and deeply into your diaphragm.

3. How To Use Cognitive Restructuring To Reduce Anger

Cognitive restructuring is a powerful psychological technique that can effectively manage and reduce anger. This method involves identifying and challenging distorted thought patterns contributing to intense emotional reactions. By restructuring these thoughts, individuals can alter their perception of a situation, leading to more balanced and constructive emotional responses. Here's a step-by-step guide on how to use cognitive restructuring to reduce anger:

Awareness and Identification: Begin by becoming aware of the thoughts associated with your anger. Pay attention to the internal dialogue and beliefs that contribute to the intensity of your emotional response.
Identify the specific thoughts that trigger your anger. These thoughts often involve cognitive distortions, such as overgeneralization, catastrophizing, or personalization.

Examine and Challenge: Evaluate the accuracy of your thoughts. Ask yourself whether your interpretations of the situation are based on factual information or distorted perceptions.

Challenge irrational and exaggerated thoughts. Consider alternative explanations for the events that evoke anger. Look for evidence that supports a more balanced and realistic perspective.

Reframe and Restructure: Replace negative and distorted thoughts with more rational and constructive alternatives. Formulate statements that reflect a balanced view of the situation.

For example, if your initial thought is, "This is unbearable; I can't stand it," reframe it as, "While this situation is challenging, I can cope with it, and there may be aspects I haven't considered."

Practice Mindfulness: Incorporate mindfulness techniques while engaging in cognitive restructuring. Stay present in the moment and observe your thoughts without judgment.

Practice deep breathing or meditation to enhance your ability to focus on the restructuring process.

Consistent Practice:

Repeat the cognitive restructuring process consistently. Changing ingrained thought patterns takes time and practice.

Monitor your progress and celebrate small victories. Recognize when you successfully apply cognitive restructuring to reduce anger in specific situations.

Seek Professional Guidance: Consider consulting with a mental health professional, such as a psychologist or counselor, who can provide guidance and support in implementing cognitive restructuring techniques. Professional assistance can offer personalized strategies and insights tailored to your unique challenges and triggers.

Let's consider a practical example of using cognitive restructuring to reduce anger:

Initial Thought: "I always mess up presentations. Everyone probably thinks I'm incompetent."

Cognitive Distortions: This thought involves overgeneralization (assuming it always happens) and mind-reading (assuming everyone thinks negatively).

Challenge and Reframe:

Challenge: Is it true that I always mess up presentations? Have there been times when I did well?

<u>Reframe:</u> While I may have faced challenges, I've also had successful presentations. Not everyone thinks negatively; some may appreciate my efforts.

Alternative Thought: "I've had both successes and challenges with presentations. I'll learn from past experiences and focus on improving."

<u>Application:</u> The next time you are faced with a presentation, consciously apply the reframed thought. Focus on the preparation and what you've learned from previous experiences rather than assuming failure.

<u>Result:</u> By restructuring your thought pattern, you approach the presentation with a more balanced mindset. This can lead to improved performance and reduced anxiety, ultimately helping manage anger associated with negative self-perceptions.

This example demonstrates how cognitive restructuring involves recognizing distorted thoughts, challenging them, and adopting more balanced perspectives. Through consistent practice, individuals can reshape their thought patterns and experience a positive impact on their emotional responses.

How To Use Expressive Writing To Reduce Anger

Expressive writing is a powerful technique that involves putting your thoughts and emotions on paper to gain insights and promote emotional well-being. Here's a guide on how to use expressive writing to reduce anger:

Step 1: Set the Scene
Create a quiet and comfortable space where you won't be disturbed. Grab a notebook or open a document on your computer—whatever feels most natural.

Step 2: Reflect on the Anger
Take a few moments to reflect on the specific situation or issue causing your anger. Identify the emotions associated with it and acknowledge the intensity of your feelings.

Step 3: Start Writing Freely
Begin writing without worrying about grammar, structure, or punctuation. Let your thoughts flow naturally onto the page. Express everything you feel, whether it's anger, frustration, disappointment, or confusion.

Step 4: Dig Deeper
As you write, try to delve into the underlying causes of your anger. Explore any past experiences, triggers, or patterns that may contribute to your emotional response. Be honest with yourself.

Step 5: Challenge Negative Thoughts
If you notice negative thought patterns emerging, challenge them within your writing. Ask yourself whether these thoughts are reasonable, and consider alternative, more balanced perspectives.

Step 6: Look for Solutions
Shift your focus toward solutions or coping mechanisms. Write about potential strategies to address the source of your anger or ways to manage your emotions more effectively in the future.

Step 7: Reflect on Positive Aspects
Conclude your writing session by reflecting on positive aspects of your life or the situation. Identify aspects you're grateful for or positive steps you can take.

Step 8: Review and Reflect
After completing your expressive writing, take some time to read through what you've written. Reflect on the insights gained and any shifts in perspective. This

process can provide a clearer understanding of your emotions.

Step 9: Repeat as Needed
Expressive writing is most effective when practiced regularly. Make it a habit to engage in this process whenever you feel overwhelmed by anger or other intense emotions.

Example:
Initial Anger: "I can't believe they treated me like that in the meeting. It's so unfair!"

Expressive Writing: "Today's meeting was frustrating. I felt disrespected when my ideas were dismissed. This reminded me of past experiences where my contributions were undervalued..."

CONCLUSION

And thus, you've reached the conclusion of your exploration into Dialectical Behavioral Therapy. Hopefully, as you've reached the end of this book, you've gained valuable insights into how these principles can serve as guiding lights on your journey through life. Always remember, the essence lies in being both accepting and open to change simultaneously. Acknowledge that, at times, embracing forthcoming changes is crucial. Recognize that there are moments when you must simply accept the unfolding events around you, and in contrast, times when you possess the agency to instigate change.

By keeping this in mind, you come to understand your intrinsic power. You realize that you indeed have the ability to initiate the transformations you seek. You comprehend that by employing the processes and tools at your disposal, you pave the way for success.

Undoubtedly, this therapy can pose challenges for some individuals. It might be demanding and, in certain respects, even painful. It requires delving into some of your deepest wounds. Navigating through this process entails reclaiming your life without letting emotions dictate it. The journey involves understanding what expectations are realistic, and it equips you with strategies to better cope with the world. Through DBT practice, you grasp the control you have over yourself. You learn that you possess the power to reshape your thoughts and feelings, thereby stabilizing your behaviors. Regardless of your past struggles or the duration of your challenges, understanding the essence of DBT can lead you to success.

Recall how mindfulness can aid in accepting the present reality. It assists you in recognizing your current emotional state and the sensations accompanying it. Mindfulness enables you to accept the world for what it is, unveiling the truth as you navigate your healing journey. Embracing mindfulness proves crucial in enhancing your ability to cope with various aspects of life.

Recall the lessons from distress tolerance, emphasizing how it empowers you to create distance from the pain you experience. Keep in mind the array of methods at your disposal, such as visualization, altering your breathing patterns, or engaging in grounding activities. These techniques serve as mental distractions, aiding you in tolerating the challenges you face. The acceptance of your current circumstances allows you to consistently apply these tools.

Never forget the insights gained from emotional regulation, offering you a comprehensive understanding of how to exert control over your reactions. Recognize that controlling your own responses is a way to influence the world around you. While you may not dictate the external outcomes, acknowledging that you've positively impacted your own actions is empowering.

Lastly, bear in mind the significance of interpersonal effectiveness when engaging with the world. It shapes how you interact with friends and those in your immediate environment. Positive and constructive interactions enhance your relationships, providing opportunities for self-improvement. Taking control of your behaviors equips you with the capability to navigate the complexities of the world more adeptly.

By recognizing your inherent power to both accept and change simultaneously, you unlock the potential of implementing the principles outlined in DBT. Embracing the tenets of DBT requires acknowledging and accepting the world, including the stressors and pain you may encounter. This acknowledgment allows you to understand that acceptance is sometimes the most appropriate response. Simultaneously, it empowers you to alter your reactions to the people and situations in your environment. The mastery of both acceptance and change is pivotal for witnessing the positive transformations you aspire to achieve.

To fully integrate these principles into your life, make them regular fixtures in your repertoire. Ensure that these tools and concepts are readily available and utilized whenever relevant. Consistent implementation of these processes, irrespective of external circumstances, will enable you to instigate the desired changes and foster personal growth. The ongoing journey of self-improvement opens up new possibilities that may have previously gone unnoticed. Embrace this growth and be willing to move towards the positive changes that await you.

I appreciate your time and dedication to exploring the content of this book. My hope is that you've discovered valuable methods to effectively manage stress. Implementing these newfound techniques should ideally yield positive results, enhancing your ability to navigate the challenges of the world around you.

If you found this book beneficial, I kindly invite you to share your thoughts by leaving a review on Amazon. Your opinions, insights, and experiences are highly valued, and your feedback contributes to the ongoing improvement of this work. Thank you for considering this, and I genuinely appreciate your engagement with the material.

DR. ANNA K.O JONES